D1030009

LOVE BEYOND PAIN

"So faith, hope, love abide, these three;
but the greatest of these is love."
I. Corinthians 13:13 (RSV)

LOVE BEYOND PAIN

Mysticism within Christianity

by
Frederick Sontag

PAULIST PRESS
New York/Ramsey, N.J./Toronto

Library of Congress
Catalog Card Number: 76-44928

ISBN: 0-8091-1998-6

Published by Paulist Press
Editorial Office: 1865 Broadway, N.Y., N.Y. 10023
Business Office: 545 Island Road, Ramsey, N.J. 07446

Printed and bound in the
United States of America

Contents

**For
Mary and Dave
and
their families**

Happy the gentle:
they shall have the earth
for their heritage

Matt. 5:4

Preface

Love, not reason, is the world's great motive force—and also its greatest source of difficulty. Thus, the chief problem for any age is to understand both the emotions and will of humankind. When this can be done, we perhaps can design a program of reform that leads to the constructive rather than the destructive use of these volatile powers. The premise of modern philosophy was that reason needed reform and improvement, but in proposing this reconstruction, the ability of reason to carry out its own reformation was never challenged. Nor was the mind's prejudice in favor of inner-directed ego-satisfaction ever properly exposed. Now that we are at the climax of the technological age, we have watched human reason develop to its full capacity, but we have also noted reason's inherent lack of concern over whether it is employed for destructive or constructive projects.

When we think of mysticism we think of the desire to transcend the limitations of thought by using reason in order to press it to a state beyond itself. Today we should be in a position to realize that mysticism can just as well mean something different: the reform of the emotions and the release of the will; that is, the mystic may desire an emptying of the self rather than just a reform of the mind so that it is stripped of all sensuous content. Today mysticism should have a different goal.

Love is a blessing, but it is a mixed blessing, since often it is as destructive and entangling as it is releasing and creative. Thus, our problem is to reform love so that it may be, if not without pain, then at least beyond pain. To accomplish this involves more than our merely pushing to transcend reason.

In attempting to explore our need and the improved state we seek, I first reviewed the Western mystical tradition from Plato to the present day. My aim was not to provide the reader with a historical survey; such already exists. My goal was to de-

1

termine whether our own mystical tradition could offer insight into the present problems we have with love.

In a time when Eastern thought has been growing in attraction, the chief mystery is why the West's own mystical tradition so often remains unexplored. In spite of the use of different images, there actually is little in the East that is not also found in the accumulated experience of the West. Of course, the simple explanation for this neglect of Western mysticism is that the Rationalist, Enlightenment, Empiricist schools all united in rejecting any mysticism and took their stand on reason as supreme. Christian theology often accepted this philosophical restriction. Thus, any dissatisfaction with the outcome of the goals of the Age of Reason or the Enlightenment forced us to the East in order to discover what was missing in our own heritage.

In trying to carry out this exploration of mysticism in the West, I, by a stroke of good fortune, was offered the chance to go to Japan to study for several months. Thus, I could review the West while living and studying in the East. As a novice in Eastern philosophy, what I have written here is not at all an essay on Buddhist thought. That would be presumptuous, and there is need neither for one more Western expert on the East nor one more enthusiast for a culture not one's own. This Western rush to the East is somewhat ironic, too, when you discover that the whole of the East seems caught in a fantastic movement to Westernize rapidly. Thus, the Westerner is found to be more sympathetic to ancient Eastern wisdom than, say, a modern Japanese industrialist or student radical. Nevertheless, let this "exchange admiration society" exist and run its course. The value of writing about Western thought while experiencing its Eastern counterpart is still an extraordinarily stimulating experience. The discerning reader should discover all sorts of Eastern contrasts and illustrations breaking in from time to time in a way that, hopefully, clarifies our own problems in the West.

Those who made this fruitful experience possible are many and deserve much thanks. My good friend Professor Masao Abe of Nara University first suggested this Eastern venture and provided the necessary introductions. Professor Masatoshi Doi,

Director of the NCC Center for the Study of Japanese Religions, graciously consented to serve as my host and provided the Center Library as a place to work and read in quiet surroundings. The Japan Society for the Promotion of Science made the venture possible by offering me a grant under their visiting professorship program.

Most of this book was shared in rough draft with a "seminar" of my colleagues brought together at regular intervals for discussion. This group included, in addition to Professors Abe and Doi, Professor Hideo Yuki of Doshisha University, Professor Shojun Bando of Otani University and Professor Shizuteru Ueda of Kyoto University. Without their stimulation and expert criticism, this book would be much weaker than it is. All were generous both in spending time in conversation and in establishing informative contacts for me.

If Japan is becoming "more Western than the West," those who have visited Kyoto know that it remains—at least as much as is possible—a city of beauty, tradition, and ancient customs. To visit the temples and gardens and shrines and palaces is itself a full-time occupation, and we were fortunate to be there to see the transition from winter to summer. If the full beauty of the cherry blossom lasts only a few days, its brief glory may remind us how quickly we must look if we want to catch the ancient spirit beneath the rapid and increasingly harsh industrialization in Japan. It is a country of strong contrasts.

Our stay from March until July of 1974 gave us only a little time to try to discover how life is lived there, but our contact was long enough to make us realize that almost every generalization one is prone to make about Japan proves too shallow in these fast-changing times. Theirs is a pluralistic culture, perhaps in many ways more heterodox and eclectic than the United States. Like all exploding cultural scenes, it is hard to catch and make stand still, but certainly it is stimulating to try.

The secretaries of the Center, Miss Tanaka and Miss Makino, were generous in helping a stranger and a newcomer with the 1,001 tasks that are so hard to negotiate alone. Professor and Mrs. William Doub, who led the University of Colorado study seminar in Kyoto, were tireless in trying to lead us further into Japanese life, and Mr. Michael Hofmann, an artist studying sumie or brush painting, was invaluable in conducting us to out-of-the-way places. The Rev. and Mrs. Aasulv Lande, special missionaries from Norway, were kind in their personal hospitality. My own colleague from Pomona College, Professor Margaret Dornish, made an excellent companion with whom to share impressions, since Eastern Religions are her special field. Mrs. Kazuko Nakijima of the Doshisha University faculty, who lived in Claremont for a time, was generous in welcoming us to her home city, Kyoto, and Mr. Yoichi Tsuchiya of the Fujita Travel Service was untiring in his use of time to help us get around in a strange land. My friend and fellow student of both Zazen and Kyoto, Alexander Eliot, read the manuscript in rough draft and is responsible for many clarifications in its form.

Miss Eiko Oklguchi typed all of the rough draft of the essay, and Professor Inouye Masana kept our enthusiasm for Japan in perspective by offerings of sake and conversation. Most impressive of all to me personally, perhaps, were Yumeko Ozeki, Yuriko Ito, and Hiroko Imai, whom I watched from my desk window as they worked each morning with a group of retarded preschool children. Their effort to draw these children into greater personal expression out of their partly locked minds was certainly, day after day, the most graphic example of how love can move beyond pain.

Kyoto, Japan

PART ONE

I

Mysticism within Christianity

For now we see in a mirror dimly, but then face to
face. Now I know in part; then I shall understand
fully, even as I have been fully understood.

I Corinthians 13:12 (RSV)

A. Temporary Mysticism

We must recognize that mysticism has meant and can
mean many things. Thus it is important to be clear about just
how the word mysticism is being used before one can evaluate
its influence. However, if mysticism knows no one definition,
this situation of fluidity also allows us no final solution.

In a minimal sense, all religions involve some degree of
mysticism. If one is not completely secular, one seeks either to
change the natural self or to achieve a transcendence of nature's
present limits. Thus, the religious seeker admits both the possibility of a transformed self and the existence of a realm different from that immediately perceived. If this is granted, how
far you go beyond nature becomes a question of degree. It
depends on how fully nature and reason's processes admit of
being gone beyond, and whether this involves us in seeking a
radically different form of existence and knowing.

The first caution that must be introduced about mysticism's role within Christianity involves the inevitable "practical" side to Christian experience. That is, for many Christians,
life is not an intellectual quest but simply a matter of inducing a
change in personal orientation and behavior. Of course, the contrast is a subtle one, because every mystic also seeks personal
change. Otherwise, he or she would have no reason to try to
transcend the natural order as it is given to all of us. The difference lies more in a matter of approach. Christians are con-

7

vinced that they may experience the change of conversion without either a prior intellectual quest or undergoing any specific discipline. They do not feel the need to assess the transformation or to elucidate its metaphysical basis. On the other hand, every identifiable mystic seeks such transformation through his or her own personal effort, and the intellect has a key role to play in this quest—even if the first aim is to quiet its assertiveness (e.g., by Zazen or the Koan).

Of course, in point of fact numerous mystics have played a role in Christian history. Their lives and writings are inextricably bound up with its total missionary effort and internal development. The consequence is that mystics form a minor—if crucial—Christian impulse. Their lives act as a counterbalance to a complete secularization, rather than forming a necessary essence and unavoidable part of what is required of every Christian. Of course, to say this leaves open the whole question of whether the mystical strains in Christian history were imported from outside, rather than having been inspired by its founder. In any case, the influence of mysticism on what Christianity has become is undeniable.

Perhaps what needs to be said is that mysticism has shaped a part of some important strains of Christian experience and doctrine, but it stops short of becoming the ultimate and singular goal of every Christian. The mystical quest seems to be a means rather than an end, whereas it can be a self-contained enterprise for the devoted follower of mystical ways. The identification or union with God may be an end in itself. One question was crucial to early Christian discussion and is still central to Christian self-understanding: Is personal transformation self-achieved? Is transcendence a matter of developed knowledge or the result of disciplined practice? Does it come to the individual from outside one's own efforts as a gift (a grace) requiring powers superior to the human, i.e., God's?

No single solution to this question of human powers vs. God's is possible. The various Christian groups have defined themselves by their position on this issue, e.g., Luther's justification by faith alone. In spite of this, it is possible to assert that orthodox Christianity has never placed salvation totally within human power, whether self-achieved or the result of following instruction from a master. Furthermore, the individual self is never the goal of any sought-for transformation. True, vast numbers of Christians are in fact selfish in their religious pursuits, but the fact remains that our instructions run counter to this. Greater service to others is the only acceptable motive for seeking or granting anyone release to a life beyond nature.

What is most important is the "temporary" nature of the Christian's involvement with mystical ways. Of course, any given individual Christian may seek a mystical state as a final end. Nothing prevents self-centered Christian pursuits, but the point is that the founding documents of Christianity point in a different direction. Paul's words to the Church at Corinth, which introduced this chapter, offer a prime example. Few if any Christians have claimed to achieve a perfectly "enlightened" state in this present existence. The complete fulfillment of Christian promises always waits for a future expected radical upheaval. Human reconstruction depends on a prior transformation in all of nature.

Given the event of the crucifixion, it is hard to claim that even Jesus achieved a final release from suffering and ego limitations during his earthly life. Otherwise, the traditional expected "second coming" is without meaning. Because Jesus' work is not yet complete, no Christian can expect to achieve a full new life now, that is, until the world's structure is altered at some future time. Most important, when that anticipated day arrives the Christian confidently expects all mystery to be overcome. God may transcend our grasp now, but he will not ultimately. The restrictions on God's intelligibility to us are temporary, and they are due to present natural structures which are destined to be broken. At that time both God and the self can be known directly. Neither necessarily transcends rational grasp, but both do so now in an interim time.

It makes all the difference in the world whether we treat mysticism's attempt to transcend human restrictions as a temporary measure for partial improvement now, or whether we see it as revelatory of the fact that Being itself is either structureless or is characterized by forms radically other than those given to us in nature. For instance, "emptiness" is an important concept in most mystical thought, although it may take different forms. With Meister Eckhart we have the notion of the "waste land" as characteristic of our experience of God at its center. With Plotinus, we strive for the One beyond distinction and expression as the source of all. In contrast, far from being contentless or beyond expression, God as Jesus experiences him seems both familiar and structured.

To be sure, any reading of the New Testament reveals its mystical aspects. How can the "kingdom" be now within each person and yet something still to come? How can believers actually share in Jesus' life, be united with their lord and all other disciples, while still remaining themselves? And finally we have the question that forms the doctrine of the trinity: how can Jesus and the Father be "one," so that those who see Jesus have seen the Father, when neither statement is true in a literal sense? We do not deny that there are many aspects of Christian teaching that exceed our grasp and require concentrated study, such as learning a discipline of meditation, if we want to penetrate the secret any further. The issue is whether the mystification is temporary and can be expected eventually to disappear.

This conclusion is complicated by the fact that any student of the mystical way who achieves enlightenment also penetrates the obscuring veil and finally "understands." However, usually this achievement is said to be beyond communication, except that one can direct another to follow along a proper path. Christianity, on the other hand, sees only a temporary and not an ultimate rational restriction on our grasp of what in itself is capable of full communication. This claim of the intelligible communicability of God or ultimate reality is crucial. If it is not possible, the whole nature of our religious pursuit is altered. Love is the key factor in all this, and it will be explored more fully in the next chapter. If God's ultimate attitude toward us is revealed to be and accepted as love, our striving toward mystical love is not eliminated, but at least it is cast in a new light.

Love, as forming the core of God's expression toward humankind and as characteristic of God's experience of his own nature, requires certain structures for its possibility. Emotion must lie at the center of God's being, perhaps as something that needs to be contained but is not ultimately eliminated. Emotional life is a fundamental attribute of the divine. It is not simply, as Spinoza thought, a by-product of reason's struggle for understanding, which disappears just to the extent that we succeed. And, if emotion has an ultimate independence from control by reason, will is required for its command. Thus, for God to love requires that concrete and personal structures characterize his nature. He is personal, not just temporarily so or in his various expressions, but ultimately as he knows and governs his own life.

If all this is so, is it only an accidental intrusion that mystical thought and practice have characterized Christian history at all? No, on the contrary they have an essential place as a corrective, even if they should never dominate Christian experience. The reverse side of this coin is that all mystical ways which exceed reason's grasp are temporary. However, a full understanding of Christianity's meaning and its God is not possible now. Even if we expect (hope) to see God fully one day, our vision now is inescapably dim. All progress in the Christian life, therefore, rests on a struggle with that veil, coupled with a personal and disciplined effort to improve the follower's life now. The aim is to release Christians, if only partially, for fuller service through developing their increased insight.

Until the completion of this promised Christian transformation, the disciple is forced to live close to the mystic way. At least that is a route some may wish to explore, while others pursue more immediate and practical means to increase the power of their gospel. Since Jesus offered no exact manual, although Loyola and others wrote down more specific rules, the Christian struggles for increased insight into the meaning of faith by following paths wherever they are found. Since Christianity did not spring new and full blown on the scene, but developed slowly out of Israel's long and varied religious tradition, it can never claim that all religious awakening is confined to some one prescribed form. Christianity was born heterodox and eclectic. Judaism's inextricable involvement opens Christian experience to search the whole world for added light.

Quite unfortunately, Christianity's missionary injunction to go out into the whole world to preach the gospel (and, we should not forget, to heal the sick also) is sometimes taken as a license to ignore the ways and insights of other religions. It leads some zealots to claim an ultimate and singular truth for Christianity and thus its right to replace all other institutional religions. However, we should remember Saint Paul's statement that even if ultimately we will see God fully, we are currently restricted to a dim vision. Thus, we know that all claims to certainty now are un-Christian by nature. Accepting this enforced uncertainty, we cannot afford to pass up any offered avenue of insight, and our preaching must also be a listening to the experience of those whom we wish to reach. Similarly, healing requires a sensitive awareness of the strengths and weaknesses of the patient if we hope to diagnose spiritual illness properly.

Moreover, God's unexpected appearance in Jesus of Nazareth does not, for the Christian who accepts it, end the matter there. Quite specifically, this is because Jesus withdrew with his work uncompleted, much to the consternation of his followers. We are told that God must appear again, since any hope which is empty remains unfulfilled. The time and the form of the divine reappearance are left vague, apparently intentionally so. Therefore, no Christian can be certain that another religious insight, e.g., Buddhism, is not crucial to his own spiritual fulfillment. The uncertainty still surrounding God's intentions leads some Christians to explore mystical lore. They do so not with a certainty but always with the possibility that God may appear again to man in other places.

B. Transformation in Place

One common characteristic of all religions is the phenomenon of looking back to the life of its founder, or founders. The disciple does this in an attempt to alter his or her own lifestyle in an effort to imitate the original way. New religions seem to arise when new charismatic figures arrive whose lives and actions and words are used as a model and directive for others. Eventually, however, our imitations of this life become blurred or degenerate or corrupt. Then the religious movement dies, if it is not revived by a reformation. That is, it must be called back to a vision of the original word and life-style of its charismatic founder, now once again rendered into a more pure form after the lapse. Thus, Christians cannot consider mysticism's place in their own lives and religious search without asking what part it may have played for Jesus.

To one used to studying contemplative mystical figures, e.g., the historical Buddha, the first thing which strikes one is how "unmystical" the life of Jesus appears. True, some such elements are present: the transfiguration, Jesus' forty days in the wilderness, the agonized prayer in the garden before his arrest. But what drives us toward mysticism is his annoying indirection in discussing himself, and also his preference for parables and symbolic rather than direct forms to express his message. Jesus' ability to perform miracles and his possession of supernatural powers also mark him as a not-natural man. Yet, all of these aspects fall short of marking him as a genuine mystic model.

Why? Jesus clearly feels that the religious practice of his day is partially corrupt, or at least it does not live up to its authentic message. He decries this ecclesiastical corruptness, just as he denounced religious charlatanism, but he does not withdraw from society or formal religion. Neither does he develop any form of meditation or transrational discipline which can then become a pattern for his disciples to imitate. Rather, his life-style takes the form of healing, of concern for others, and of preaching his message in a rather simple style and in a form not beyond the grasp of anyone. In fact, his words are perhaps intended more for the simple than the wise. If his is an esoteric teaching, it is so only because it has not been completely fulfilled, rather than because it requires uncommon learning to grasp it.

As has been admitted, not every saying of Jesus is easy or obvious. The Gospel of John is often set aside by those who prefer the less hidden forms of expression of the synoptic gospels. Yet these more difficult sayings, as John expresses them (e.g., "I am the way and the truth and the life"), must be accepted as part of Jesus' intended revelation. To struggle with them does take us closer to mystical modes of interpretation, however. The simple fact that we have multiple pictures of Jesus and not one, some more obscure in their phrasings than others, dooms Christian followers to explore any avenue of insight likely to open the "true Christ" to them.

Although a few of Jesus' references hint at hidden meanings that must be decoded, on the whole he does not claim that ultimate truth is beyond either his or our utterance. Rather, he tends to say that the truth is near at hand, often overlooked just because of its deceptive simplicity. Such a teaching has echoes in other mystical literature; Zen enlightenment usually is triggered by a mundane event. Yet the systematic point remains: the truth about God and the world and man can be communicated. And Jesus claimed to have done this by his word *and* by his action. We might or might not understand it all; his message might or might not be effective for any individual. But that fault lies more in the condition of the recipient than in any characteristic about ultimate truth that places it beyond the rational grasp of the average person.

Since God is the most important object in religion, as well as the ultimate concern for both religious understanding and improved action, it is Jesus' manner of speaking about God which more than anything else marks him off from the normal image of the mystic's way. Like early Israel, most mystics, e.g., Bonaventure or Dionysius the Areopagite, are reluctant either to approach or to speak about God directly. The mystic becomes the mystic because he or she thinks that abnormal or unusual means, plus new disciplines and ways of speaking or behaving are necessary if God is to be approached or nature transcended. Ordinary rational tools seem ultimately inadequate to the mystic, and so new techniques must be developed by stern discipline and hard apprenticeship to a master.

It is at this point that Jesus' attitude stands in its sharpest contrast. His references to God are simple and direct. "Father" is the intimate term he most often uses. His interpersonal mode of address, and thus the assumption of God's personal attributes, is unmistakable. If God is centrally and ultimately personal in his nature, anthropomorphic references are appropriate, and full and complete disclosure is possible. If God's nature finally is apprehensible in a human form, little mystery will remain in the long run. However, the veil on God's face may continue in the short run, since the disclosure is not yet complete. Jesus' personal references are merely forecasts of how we can come to know God. They are not yet a factual statement about how God is presently known.

Here is the core of Christianity, and it cannot be set aside. For those who accept it, it is a claim to the full disclosure of God's nature and intentions. This much being said, we must quickly add that the disclosure is not yet complete; it is only attested to by certain acts, e.g., Jesus' resurrection. We do not and cannot experience its complete realization in the present state of the world. The Christian *hopes* to know God fully in an unspecified future day, and Jesus' intimate relationship serves as a model more for the future than the present. However, the hope is not simply hope against hope; it is attested to by Jesus' life and statements. Furthermore, the disclosed core of the divine nature is love. And if this is true, the Christian need not rest simply in hope but can move beyond it. In the present age, however, the revelation is not without its mystery, and so mystical pursuits have an expedient function.

To say all this might seem simple and to put an end to the matter. It would, if only Jesus had spoken directly, if he had communicated his doctrine clearly and formulated a consistent technical theology in his own words, rather than depending on varied interpreters and an oral transmission. However, such is not the case. Our problems in interpreting the scriptures lead us as easily to a mystical kabbala as to the more optimistic and rational approach of "form criticism" and historical scholarship. Given varied and not-fully-clear scriptural documents, if we put aside the pride of nineteenth-century scholarship to achieve a final rendering, we can never hope for one authenticated reading. Thus, mystical attempts to uncover a hidden and a secret teaching always remain an open possibility and are a temptation to anyone seeking religious answers.

Jesus' preference for the use of parable and symbol can be interpreted as an attempt to communicate with the unlearned in forms they can easily grasp. If Jesus' message is universally open and not restricted to some esoteric group who alone are privileged to understand, this is both an obvious possibility and a partial explanation. Noting his indirect and thus imprecise if colorful mode of expression in the symbol, the visual image and the story, we realize that these are also at the heart of the mystic's mode of instruction, e.g., the Hasidic communication via story. The mystic's purpose may be different; Jesus' motives may be merely provisional and practical and democratic. The mystic, on the other hand, may speak thus because the transrational nature of reality requires it, and also because no other means of enlightenment is possible either now or in any future.

If the way one prays indicates what that person thinks God is like, we must take the "Lord's Prayer" very seriously in assessing Jesus' "mystical" inclinations. The prayer is simple, direct, short. It assumes that the one addressed has a will and goal which he will eventually enact. Breaking out of these limitations does not seem to be the aim of Jesus' prayer. Long ritual procedures and extreme discipline are explicitly avoided. Neither union with God nor self-emptying in any traditional sense are the goals, although it is clear that prayer aims to lift the one who prays beyond the narrow confines of one's own self and will. One could describe Jesus' reported prayer life as a "mild mysticism." It contains some strands of mystical transcendence, but it does not evidence a "complete mysticism" for his inner life.

This brings us to what might be called the Christian ideal of "transcendence in place." Some mystical pursuits require a radically altered life-style and a break with normal society. Christianity does aim to transform the individual, and it claims the power to accomplish this, but it still insists that this alteration takes place "in the world." Of course, in pursuing the Christian goal of "new life" some may resort to esoteric practices or radical disciplines. The point is that Christianity does not itself require this as its sole means of advancement in new life. However, an outreach to redress human need is enjoined upon us. This required outward opening does not eliminate the cloister, but it does put it under severe question. The demand is

that any isolated life show both how it fulfills more than the individual's goals and how it carries out the injunction to heal the
sick.

Christian renewal can be sought for and expressed in many
ways. Any individual may adopt a certain discipline or choose a
severe path of self-denial, but all Christian life is not bound to
that form. Christianity does join all mystics in asserting the
necessity to break the shell of the immediate world that binds
us, but the world we want to break through to cannot be totally
different from our natural order nor does it lie beyond our normal grasp. The Christian's desired "kingdom" is already within
the present world, and thus it can be sought and expressed
within it. Qualities of the desired new life are already immediately around us. "Consider the lilies of the field." The aim is to
release these suppressed aspects to full expression without shutting people away from life or turning them from the world
before us.

"Transformation in place" claims to alter the religious
seeker without demanding a break with the natural order. It
directs one's attention to a new world, but then it returns one
immediately to serve the present world's needs with greater effectiveness and commitment. Like any mystic way, achieving
this desired change and the required infusion of power depends
upon breaking those bonds of the natural world that restrain the
human spirit. This involves contact with a Holy Spirit which is
not readily discernible by those who dominate, or are dominated by, the powers that presently shape the course of the world.
Both the mystic and the Christian seek release from a stultify-
ing and stunting natural life. The issue between us comes over
what extremes are demanded if we are to achieve this. The question is whether removal from society is necessary, and what use
should be made of any heightened spiritual power that results.

In trying to assess the role that mysticism has played and
can play within Christianity, we might conclude that, except for
the goad of its mystics, Christianity might forget that its goal is
to transcend the world rather than to accommodate to it. On
the other hand, Christianity itself is not simply another form of
mystical doctrine. In fact, it differs on important points, e.g.,

the selfhood and familiar nature of God. Since "mysticism" covers a broad range of views itself, it may overlap Christianity at many points. Christianity will at times develop along lines close to mystical doctrine, e.g., in the Gospel of John or with Meister Eckhart. If "mysticism" means the necessity and the attempt to transcend the natural order if human fulfillment is to be achieved, to be a Christian is to be at least minimally a mystic.

When it is appraised against the mystical tradition, whether East or West, Christianity can define its role more clearly. This is probably what happened at the time of its inception in relation to the mystical lore then current. As the early Christian community learned how they differed from current esoteric cults, they came to understand what it meant to be "Christian." Without this, any religion falls into idolatry. That is, it too easily comes to espouse some immediate human achievement or cultural goal, rather than pressing beyond natural human concern to find God and to discover his will. Since neither God nor his will is immediately obvious, the mystical quest with its demanded purification and discipline protects us against the illusion of accepting pleasurable cultural attractions as if they were ultimate. However, the basic goal of "transformation in place" always returns Christians to the spot where they began. It enjoins them to work within the world by using their renewed power in a natural setting. Of course, any given mystical doctrine, e.g., Zen, may affirm this goal too. Thus, any conflict which may arise between Christianity and other religions is not a necessary one. Rather, it is a matter of Christianity's realizing what its gospel does or does not allow it to affirm and where its newly realized power for action is to be directed.

II
Beyond Hope

A. A Theology of Experience

To try to follow "the mystical way" is an individual endeavor; it overlaps the aims of Christianity but is never identical. However, it is enlightening to note that both Christianity and mysticism share one common and fundamental point. Any venture into the discipline required by the mystical search involves more than the intellect and cannot be judged solely by rational criteria. The evaluation is based on the practical results of its success in changing the life-style and depth of experience of the individual. In the East, philosophy and religion have always been joint enterprises. This is because any pursuit of one of the forms of mystical enlightenment requires the kind of life-style and endeavor which in the West we classify as "religion."

Few philosophies in the West require a transcendence of ordinary experience. Few aim to open wider realms for the mind and to change the life of the searcher. In fact, particularly in the continental Rationalist and British Empirical traditions of modern philosophy, the aim has been to make philosophy an enterprise totally based on empirical experience as it is given and reason as it normally operates. Not all Western philosophy has insisted on this. In other parts of our tradition, philosophy can be expanded to include religious or even mystical endeavor.

Christianity, on the other hand, necessarily tests itself by its ability to change radically (that is, to liberate) the individual follower. The New Testament documents are full of Jesus' reference to the unacceptability of mere verbal or intellectual confession. "By their fruits shall they be known." Jesus' disciples are not merely those who say "Lord, Lord" but those who do his Father's will. The injunction is not to think differently but to go out in the world to preach and heal. The necessary conditions to achieve this desired change or conversion are the repentance of former ways and a forgiveness that releases one to new life.

Thus, the aim is transformation and the ultimate test for it is redirected action and expanded vision, plus the release of full human potential. All this unites Christianity to mystical practice, although neither to any one way nor to any assertion that mystical discipline offers the "only way." The needed transformation and release may come to the individual from outside, perhaps as a gift that is not directly proportional to one's efforts. Yet to say this ties Christianity to a "theology of experience," although it may not be what the British tradition means by empirical experience-as-given. Instead, the transformation of behavior is the only valid criterion for the authenticity of any doctrine.

However, the way "love" can enter into this process is particularly important. From studying the history of love's treatment in philosophy, we know what wherever love is given serious attention as a philosophical concept that can produce insight, e.g., Plato's Phaedrus, emotion becomes philosophically important to those who would achieve new insight. Philosophy is no longer strictly a matter of rational endeavor. Love changes the one it falls upon. Even if not all of its forms are enlightening and even if some are destructive, the resulting alteration and the centrality of emotion are undeniable. The philosopher cannot pursue the goal of insight and still hope to remain unmoved. Prior personal change may even be a condition for achieving insight.

It is particularly interesting to consider all this in relation to Jesus' own announced test for discipleship. In this way, he said, people will know that you are my disciples, that you love one another. We can all share the same hope and recite the same creed. We may even share similar intellectual convictions, but the central test of discipleship is still measured by our altered affection. Can one love freely now where formerly hate or indifference ruled? You may follow Wittgenstein's philosophical program and not necessarily love all fellow Wittgensteinians, but such is not the case with Christianity. The only acceptable evidence for belief is altered behavior evidenced by a changed emotional life and a new directional flow of love.

To feel pain is not necessarily part of the philosopher's life. In fact, some philosophies, e.g., Epicureanism, are built on an elaborate insight as to how pain can be avoided by observing the proper discipline. It is significant that love plays no prominent role in either Stoicism or Epicureanism, for we now know that love involves pain, at least until the present conditions of human life are changed. Every mystic, e.g., St. John of the Cross, testifies to the pain and anguish one must endure as part of the quest and one's own trials of purification. Thus, the Christian injunction to love all people, even one's enemies, as well as God is bound to bring continual pain. Such frail human love-objects are far less beautiful than Plato's forms, but the attention of Christians is directed more toward the sordid condition of people's lives than away from it to some ideal beauty.

A mystic may seek eventual release from emotion, and perhaps achieve this by transcending the natural limits of the world. He or she may even hope to occupy a position beyond the sway of emotion, e.g., Satori, but this is not the Christian goal nor does the assigned direction of Christian emotion allow it. To be sure, the follower of Zen may be active in the world too and deeply involved in emotion, but the difference is that the Christian never ceases to be affected by compassion for human suffering. Christians hope to find a base of confidence so that they are not overwhelmed and can operate effectively. But they are themselves constantly involved and they must respond. Even if the Zen monk can say the same thing, there still remains the issue of what happens to the self and the role of God in this process.

In Christian biography the relationship between conversion and violence is clear. Saint Paul is the well-known classic instance. His early involvement in the physical violence of killing Christian followers is connected to his sudden and radical conversion. He came to love exactly that which he formerly hated with such intensity. Eric Erickson has a similarly enlightening study in *Young Man Luther* which links pent-up passion and intense emotion with the suddenness of Luther's conversion and psychological change. A Christian, once converted, may adopt or follow certain practices of mysticism as a way to deepen spirituality, but he or she is not often first won over to Christianity by the slow and necessarily demanding rigors of any mystical discipline.

In the recent example of the Berrigan brothers, and in Hanna Arendt's study *On Revolution*, we recognize the connection between conversion and the kind of tension that builds up slowly. Increasing tension gradually and silently does prepare us for a change that finally bursts forth in revolution. Arendt correctly sees that some emergent revolutionary passions are destructive. They undercut their own hope of providing a permanent liberation to larger numbers just because their violence cannot contain itself and so leads to cyclical and spreading destruction. Thus, as a movement that hopes to create a revolution in the behavior of human beings, Christianity must recognize the close connection between violence and conversion, but it hopes to direct this force constructively by the dominance of love over hate.

A.D. Nock's study of *Conversion*[1] analyzes the factors that give a revolution in behavior its compelling force. The powers of change with which people must deal are uncanny. That is, they defy easy rational assimilation, and this is much more true when emotions are admitted as a legitimate philosophical subject, rather than when philosophical analysis is restricted to the life of reason. More important, any sudden change seems to require the emergence of a prophet as its instrument. An individual left on his or her own, perhaps quietly reading Descarte's *Meditations* in the study, is not likely to undergo a radical change in direction even though Descartes desires it. A prophet is one with a profound dissatisfaction for things as they are, and fired with a new idea. Of course, to the extent that Descartes becomes such a prophet, he may also induce a radical conversion of direction.

A prophet is moved by an inner impulse to deliver this message. Those who find themselves aroused by the prophet may experience a drastic change in direction of thought or action, but this kind of dramatic figure, one who appeals to the emotions, is necessary if a radically new course is to emerge. Conversion is the reorientation of the total personality, Nock tells us. It is a turning from indifference to a conviction that the new way is right (p. 7). In this sense, it is as operative in strictly philosophical circles as it is in religious. Both require as their motive force the conviction that all former actions are bad and must be turned away from. This is what Existentialism or Logical Positivism or the Wittgensteinians have done in recent times in their move to build a philosophical following.

The power of any prophet derives from the fact that, in the people and the times around him, the emotions beneath the surface are seeking just such a form of expression as the one the new prophet fuses together. Thus, Wittgenstein could not have been successful unless philosophy was in some state of nonfertility and dissatisfaction when he arrived on the scene. Similarly, Kierkegaard was not really successful in his own time in spreading a revolution, until that day when the European experience in two world wars built people to the same state of discontent which he had felt and expressed earlier in his "thoughts out of season." Thus, the success of the change philosophers want to induce in their colleagues depends not so much on the simple and obvious truths they state as on the correspondence of their theories to the emotional substate of the day. Do the new proposals have an ability to give the felt needs a stable and analyzable form for expression? If so, the new thought can become powerful, not on its own, but due to the emotions it gives form to.

Philosophical frenzy does not appear to be as evident as religious frenzy, but the basic conditions are the same for both. The mind knows a discontent just as the spirit and the emotional life do. Being a thing of the intellect, philosophical frenzy is more verbal in its form and less obviously violent. But it is also less conscious of the forces that move beneath its surface and operate to change its convictions. For instance, note Freud's analysis of the "unconscious" which Descartes and Sartre avoid completely, since it threatens pure rationality.

Thus, the violence involved in religious conversion is simply a much more graphic and illustrative model of how change takes place than is the quieter surface of intellectual debate.

We use the mind to analyze. We explore the hidden life of the passions, as well as their surface violence, but we can only chart the special ways of the spirit by internal exploration. In any mystical way and in Christianity, these three are indissolubly wedded. Since intellect is only one part, the test of the adequacy of a doctrine lies not in intellectual assent but in the novice's altered behavior and converted emotional direction. That is, do emotions move from hate to love, from self-attention to the needs of others? Spiritual insight and a greater sensitivity to one's interior and unobserved life, these are important too. Yet for the Christian, even the fruits of the spiritual life are tested not by piety or even spirituality, but by the pattern of the new behavior that results.

The conversion experience, and its connection to violence and revolutionary change, should always be central in any Christian doctrine. Theology apparently moves steadily and rationally, but its aim and test still lie in its ability to produce and to control radical change. Now we know why Jesus took no pains to leave us with a clear and precise doctrinal statement. His design was not to please historical scholars with the finality or the openness of his doctrine to verification or authoritative control. He sought not correct doctrine alone, although that has its place, but new behavior. In such a situation, he tried to avoid leaving the impression that correct doctrine made verbally precise is the aim of Christianity. It is not as such; it is only insofar as, when stated clearly, theory provides a means to personal transformation and a conversion of emotional direction.

B. The Revolution of Love

The mood of prophets is one of expectancy. If people respond, it is because the prophets appeal to the same mood that lies latent in the mood of those who hear them and follow. They speak of what they see coming in the future, so that the prophet can be one either of foreboding or of hope. Saint Paul, in the theme passage used for this volume, speaks of the now-famous

three Christian virtues: faith, hope and love. What is of concern
to us is why, theologically speaking, he ends by asserting love to
be primary. There are purists and lovers of rigor who want to
make faith in some strict formula the sole test of orthodoxy, but
we know from Paul's classification that this is the third virtue
and should never be made first or given exclusive stress. Faith
remains a secondary, or even a tertiary, consideration.

Much theological discussion recently has centered on the
mood of hope. It is true that, in the Christian prophetic sense,
the forecast is not one of doom but of the potential for new life.
Those who use Christianity to predict the destruction of their
enemies—or of whatever they dislike—are misusing it and reversing its intended directional flow. Christianity became great
not because it prophesied much destruction, but because it offered hope for human reconstruction. However, it is often said
that those who reject the Christian message do so because they
cannot share its hope. The crucial point is that the disillusioned
ones are not able to do this because they fail to see the primacy
of love over all other considerations.

Saint Paul lists the virtues of love in his text, e.g., long suffering, but the correctness of his description is not so much the
issue. One may love love and still fail to agree to its centrality
over faith and hope or understand how love makes both possible. This is because love may be described phenomenologically
or even experienced, but its revolutionary potential can still be
overlooked. And this revolution is central to all Christian understanding. That is, if we are to have faith or are to be moved
beyond resting in hope, only love can accomplish this. This
power is not present in love's every form, yet love has the potential for a revolution in the life of human emotion. Spinoza
proposed to alter the emotions by the use of reason. Christianity
proposes to make a change in the intellect, in human conduct,
and in man's outlook, all by the use of love's potential for revolutionary change.

How is it that love can create a revolution that moves us
beyond hope? According to the Christian analysis, this released
power comes from the availability of a new understanding of
God, i.e., a "revelation." This unveiling changes our outlook on

what we find around us in the natural world and in human behavior. Thus, in an age where God is either not clearly seen or
his pursuit is neglected, the genius of the Christian approach is
restricted to a mood of hope against hope. God's new action is
the key to love's ability to produce change, so that it is God
who must be understood anew before human life can expect improvement.

No "natural God" can serve this function. If we build our
picture of God's nature from the world as we experience it, we
enter into Hume's contradiction,[2] and we are left with a God no
better and no worse than the mixed good and evil we find
around us. If we idealize God by abstracting from one side of
nature which we find to be good, we remove him from contact
with the world. His idealized nature cannot explain the difficult,
even the evil, sides of the world and humanity, and it is these
that require both explanation and religious resolution. God's
emotions must be different from our natural instincts, but how
are these divine moods to be discovered? And how can God's
emotions alter human behavior in order to move us beyond a
fixation on hope?

By his actions as well as in his words and by God's treatment of him, Jesus announced God's peculiar form of love. But
we know that this is not without its increased involvement with
pain, since it pushes us to painful human encounter. A love that
is happy enough to know no pain cannot cure pain, except
perhaps by covering it over and hoping that it will not reappear.
A love that experiences crucifixion can resolve pain, if it is not
destroyed in the process. Jesus almost lost this battle at the
crucial moment by yielding to a sense of God's abandonment of
him, as so many people have done in our contemporary age.
But God's own actions, e.g., resurrection, reversed this move
toward self-destruction. Such exposed power enabled love, as he
left it to be embodied by his disciples, to convert pain. Thus
hope is given its future substance.

It is religious suicide to demand that anyone simply believe
either in immortality or in Jesus' resurrection. Human experience does not move in that direction, that is, from belief or intellectual affirmation to a conviction in the validity of Chris-

tianity's promises. Rather, one first enters into a study of love in oneself, in others, and in God. Then, if this adventure is religiously fruitful, the Christian finds love in God to be powerful enough to overcome pain and loss, whereas human love rarely can. Human beings can make sense of the doctrine of resurrection only if, in their own experience, they find a God powerful enough to hold out against the destructive erosion of pain. We receive the right to hope, not because we simply have hope and want it, but because love, as we now experience it in God's outflow, offers a ground for hope in its power eventually to reconstruct human nature.

Is love experienced as a revolutionizing force that is capable of reversing the natural shifts of violent emotion between hatred and destruction? Only if it is can "faith" and "hope" be words whose real substance is felt. Otherwise they appear as human wishes blowing against the hurricane of the world's natural forces. The difficulty involved here is that love is all too seldom experienced in this way. It is itself full of complexities and has many sides, some destructive and distorting. The catalog of the depths of depravity to which love drives men is infinitely longer (if we want to locate and experience a real infinite in the modern world) than love's beautifying powers.

When we romanticize love, we cover over its religious depths by painting it as something purely beautiful, lovely, and sheer delight (see *Hair* or read *Playboy*). Entering into the horrors to which men's passions and loves drive them is a necessary preliminary to any Christian grasp of love's depths in God and its powerful capacities. For religious purposes, murder mysteries, horror movies, and Japanese "comic books" of violence are better preparation for experiencing the love of God than romantic novels, sentimental hymns, or even most great works of religious art—unless they capture the sense of power and awe in the divine depths. To solve love's mystery, and the mystery of how it can save as well as destroy, is to understand God, or to be understood by him.

If there can be a resolution to the pain of love, then there is ground for hope and also some reason to feel a mood of faith rather than desperation. If God's love responds to the explosive force of the passions, and if it can convert love's direction to a mode of new life without destruction or pain, then love can be seen as a revolutionary force capable of altering human life. Only those so transformed by its effects can be expected to have much hope or to place much conviction in their voiced faith. It is right to recognize that hope requires an orientation toward the future, but such a hoped-for-future will collapse if it depends only on faith for support and not on the experience of the revolutionary power of God's love.

Now we are in a position to see why religion is strongest when it is organized as a "missionary church," and why the religious spirit grows weak when it turns inward to analyze its own life or to argue over either some demand for faith or some effort to keep hope alive. To be sure, not all missionary activity is good. Significantly, this activity becomes suspect when it concentrates on trying to inculcate belief as an initial step. When we listen to Jesus' directives and attempt to spread the gospel by ministering to human needs and exhibiting a spirit of love, then the missionary church is a strong church precisely because it is experiencing and exhibiting in action what it later will seek to understand by faith. On the other hand, a non-missionary church is a troubled church, because it is turned inward to argue with itself. Thus, it necessarily fails to reduplicate the essential Christian spirit in its own life.

"Power to the people" is a cry which recently has been given new prominence in its use by revolutionary leaders. The Christian cry is much the same. Power in the world does tend to settle in aristocratic and selfish centers that stifle free movement and repress human liberation. Love has an ability, the Christian convert reports from experience, to give power to the people. Essentially this is God's power, as it is evidenced in his revolutionizing love. But the radical news of Christian preaching is that God has moved to share such power with people and to make it available for human transformation. Our power to release and transform, it asserts, depends on love for its prior release.

"We shall overcome" became a popular Negro spiritual used among civil rights leaders and demonstrators in what

Americans call the "Black revolution" of the 60s. "We shall overcome" is a Christian cry, but the next word in that song, "someday," is crucial if we are to understand it. Furthermore, we need to be clear about what it is that we will "overcome." In the present context, this would seem to be the destructive tendencies of human passions and powers. The pain accompanying love is also what Christians claim will be overcome some day, because they have experienced God's love as capable of both reversing destruction and healing pain.

In all of these aspects, we should call our age a "pre-Christian twenty-first century." That is, we are still held in a mood of expectant waiting. Our present mood is hope, Moltmann is right, but the major question is whether we can move beyond this. We live today, it turns out, in the same way that the disciples did in the pre-resurrection days after Jesus' crucifixion. Almost every hope humanity had to provide its own transformation of human life and society has faded, from prohibition to utopian societies and central social planning. Our naive religious hope in the ability of ritual and belief alone to heal has been crucified, and now the issue is whether love can break through and prevail over this natural iconoclasm. Can we find our hope destroyed that the organized Church will lead a revolution, and yet find God's love revolutionizing human hope in the experience of the pain of that death?

We wait expectantly, just as the disciples did after Calvary, hoping in Jesus' power to overcome the forces oppressing them. Christians now treat other Christians as they did in that earlier nervous era. We have not all abandoned hope, but most Christians today live and even worship without any moving conviction in the power of their own love. Neither a theological examination nor a new creed nor even a new social project will as such cure this situation. A new quest for the historical Jesus will not support a failing faith, since it is not the historical Jesus but the Jesus-of-the-future-actions who gives us any ground to trust him. Only an experience that changes the directional flow of love in our own lives, one that moves love beyond pain and reveals God as offering a love with a nonnatural capacity to revolutionize human life—only such a theology of experience can move Christians out of their present waiting mood. We are today like the women who huddled together after the crucifixion, not even knowing where Jesus is buried.

Hope left alone eventually fades. Faith intellectually affirmed, even out of natural emotional compulsion, cannot sustain itself. As Paul reports, hope ultimately will fail, and we know this to be true. Prophets rise and pass away and hope fades again, until it receives a new momentary impulse. Only love has revolutionary power. Human love has this in potential, if properly released; divine love has it in actuality, if properly revealed. Only these powers can move us beyond the natural panorama of self-love, war and pain. Can the revolutionary potency of God's love be experienced again and move us beyond our pre-resurrection mood of waiting for hope? We await the new proclaimers of this revolutionary power, i.e., the gospel.

Notes to Chapter II

1. A. D. Nock, *Conversion* (London: Oxford University Press, 1933).

2. See David Hume, *Dialogues on Natural Religion.*

III

Spiritual Exercises

A. The Dark Night

In popular sentiment, John of the Cross is perhaps most closely connected with the notion of "the dark night of the soul." The intellect and senses must undergo a radical purgation before they can hope to attain their goal of insight. In appraising such a proposed program, what we face is a question in epistemology. That is, what is the best means to knowledge, and how radical must the transformation of the mind be before it is prepared to pass beyond its present restricted state? The first issue is that of exoteric vs. esoteric knowledge. Is the access route to greater insight so rigorous and so restricted that it is open only to a few? Does it involve such drastic requirements that only some will or can make the necessary effort?

The history of philosophy (and religion) is filled with many theories of knowledge. Some try to stay close to the present human state; some require less alteration to achieve knowledge, some more. However, it is interesting to note that the major question is simply one of degree. That is, all philosophers agree that some change in the ordinary ways of human understanding is necessary. If it were otherwise, their profession would not be needed. Descartes writes about how human understanding must and can be improved, and so does Spinoza. Locke thinks we do not understand the strengths and weaknesses of our own instruments of human reasoning, and Kant proposes elaborate means for their self-analysis. Although not all philosophers agree, Plato at least is convinced that the sense world must be transcended. Thus, our problem is first to decide the degree of change required in our mode of knowing, and then we must estimate whether the reformation needed to accomplish this breakthrough is mild or radical.

31

Underlying this decision is the question that must be faced before any stable conclusion can be reached: ultimately, do we trust rationality and conceptualization? Some never question the inherited intellectual bias of the West—that we have no choice but to do so. Kant is convinced that we must all make an unalterable commitment to reason, and he is also sure that our basic task is simply to explore its structure and its depths. However, all philosophers have not agreed with this. Even if the tradition of empiricism is content to trust sense data as an ultimate standard of reliability, we still have a right to ask whether the conceptualizations of the intellect can be accepted as ultimately trustworthy and thus revelatory of truth. Partly at issue here is the question of the primacy of "discreteness," the tendency of the intellect to create distinctions and then to grasp all reality in those terms.

The intellect naturally moves first to make distinctions and then to use these modes of discreteness. That is its function, and that is its nature; but the issue is whether we ought to step back first and question this whole operation. Is our mind's innate tendency to make distinctions to be accepted as the "way to truth," or should we be more radical and ask whether reason's tendency to create distinct logical structures may be a block to truth at times? The basic issue is one of how we form our theory of knowledge. We cannot accept any proposal as obvious. First we must remain skeptical and ask what alternatives are open to us. Are some approaches to knowledge themselves subject to blind spots by their very nature? The possible necessity of passing through a "dark night" challenges us most radically. Must the intellect and the senses first be totally purged and emptied before our understanding can hope to make any progress beyond its original inherited limitations?

At this point we meet the question of the total adequacy of language as a mode of accurate expression. Even followers of the theory of "ordinary language" do not accept vague talk as it exists. Rather, all they insist on is that language as it is commonly used can be so analyzed as to provide its own standard of correction. From there, we move on to all degrees of confidence, and lack of confidence, in the ability of language to bear and to convey truth adequately. Descartes never seems to doubt the full capacity of the words he uses to contain truth, and thus he uses mental meditation uncritically as the sole tool needed to lead the mind to certainty. Plato, in his use of a dialogue technique of indirectness as well as in his reliance on myth and metaphor, represents a more cautious school. He is one of those who continue to use language to lead the mind, all the while he is sure that words do not and cannot in themselves contain truth.

Where Christian doctrine is concerned, its classical epistemological text is the prologue to the Gospel of John: "In the beginning was the Word." That is, any "logos" theology assumes the ultimate compatibility of God with rational discourse. Rationality can be used to grasp reality, because reality was first created through the mediation of rational thought as it was formed in, and thus characterizes, the divine mind. This, however, does not eliminate the possible necessity of passing through a human "dark night." The "word" that is with God and in God and then descends to become flesh after having formed the world at its beginning—such a powerful "word" involves hard thoughts and does not easily fit into any "normal" way of approaching rationality. If it is to grasp this process, human reason must first be lifted above normal conceptualization. To do this may require inducing at least a provisional "dark night" of the senses.

Because God himself speaks and has spoken, Christianity has retained an ultimate trust in our powers of communication. This it has done in spite of the verbal difficulties it has encountered, the frequent failures or distortions of speech and the evident need for individual reformation. Human speech may not be powerful and insight producing in every form, but it can be, even if in a majority of cases it involves a built-in obscurity that must be overcome. Here we run up against the question of the story form vs. straight discourse, the issue of whether verbalization can assume the mode of an effective work of art. The Hasidic tradition trusts a story told rather than analytic discourse to convey its insights. Thus, when we stress Christianity's confidence in the potential rightness of our available verbal and conceptual means, we must broaden this to include both a symbolic and a nonliteral use of language.

Are we under a necessity for each of us individually to learn to write powerfully before we can discover and then convey truth ourselves? Not all philosophers have thought so, and many methods of spiritual discipline stress silence and a strict training that seeks to break off our too-strong and uncritical dependence on conceptual thought. Yet, when we find that we must write down our experience in order to convey the beauty seen or the truth revealed, we learn that an ability to communicate is necessary to apprehension, and inarticulateness becomes a sign of confusion. Each of us needs to witness words being born in rational form and to feel in this experience the road to greater insight. Do we trust dialogue and human exchange as being necessary for truth, or is solitude really truth's last hiding place? Does the practice of writing relieve the dilemmas that confront us, so that learning the forms of adequate communication can itself break the deadlock that holds back the mind?

When we try to construct a theory of knowledge that allows for a "dark night" and thus requires spiritual discipline as the condition for acquiring knowledge, we encounter a slight paradox. Any doctrine that claims that rationality and our tendency to conceptualize must be overcome is forced to place an extraordinary importance on the powers of the mind and their abilities. The transcendence of reason must be accomplished by reason, although this paradox is not really so strange. Hume noted the same thing for those who are skeptical of reason, those who are "mystics in reverse." That is, they must use reason in order to disprove reason's validity. They must at least put confidence in one rational argument: the one that aims to deny reason's powers. Otherwise, skepticism is groundless. In order to say: "If he can control his mind he can find the way of enlightenment and all wisdom and virtue will naturally come to him,"[1] one must place an extreme importance on mental powers indeed.

D. T. Suzuki tells us: "There is a great mystery which cannot be solved on the plane of intellection. . . . The function of the intellect consists in leading the mind to a higher field of consciousness by proposing all sorts of questions which are beyond itself."[2] Yet, notice that it is the mind which is used to drive itself beyond itself. And we must ask: what kind of theory of knowledge is implied here? Evidently, it is only by thought that we can know that something lies beyond thought. If so, is such a truth really "beyond intellection," or does it simply require that intellect first be raised to a higher plane? Do we simply aim to expand and improve intellection by releasing it from its limitations? Or do we go further and claim that we really must go "beyond" the intellect itself?

The central question becomes: what is the function of the intellect; or rather, what functions is the intellect capable of assuming? Suzuki again declares the inadequacy of the intellect, of course arguing by intellectual means, as his Zen critics are quick to point out: "For Zen always aims at grasping the central fact of life, which can never be brought to the dissecting table of intellect."[3] But we must ask: what is the central fact of life, why does it transcend intellect, and how can we know that this is the case?

Buddhism often speaks of "the delusion of reasoning,"[4] but in Western theology we might transfer this into the question: "What is the status and function of reason in the divine nature?" If we could understand how God reasons, we might understand what reason can and cannot do, and also in what way human rational powers need improvement. If we grant that reason is at times "deluded," can it be trusted as a guide once it has undergone self-correction? Is the "dark night" itself still a very special process of reasoning and not simply the absence of all reason?

Hegel might be thought of as the leading exponent of the powers of reason, once it is properly, i.e., dialectically, corrected. "The systematic development of truth in scientific form can alone be the true shape in which truth exists."[5] Hegel proposes a new and intricate way in which truth must be approached, but it is by reason that this is to be done, even if it is by reason as marvelously modified. Is reality conceptually grasped, or does final truth lie beyond reason's reach, we must ask? If we are told "beyond it," we have a right to ask why, and how can this be known to be the case? We may even need to induce in ourselves a "dark night," that time when all sense experience and intellection ceases. But we still want to know: after that, will thought begin again with greater power?

After considering the issues involving the powers of conceptualization and reason, we move on to ask: How can we determine the status and the power of language to convey reality? The issue is not whether language often fails; it does. But is there any time at all when it can be an adequate conveyer? Is it inherently defective or simply in need of correction so that, if only on occasion, it can still lead some aright? Perhaps put more subtly, we need to determine whether language can be used to express the inexpressible? Saint Anselm reminds us that the term "incomprehensible" is comprehensible although that to which it refers is not. Thus, language does not need to convey literally all that it wishes to express. It is enough if it leads the mind to that position where it might discern what lies beyond itself.

This brings us to the question of how language functions as a teaching instrument. Must it, in some literal sense, contain within its own confines that which it wants to present to another mind? The Platonic use of dialogue might be contrasted here with the Zen problem or Koan. Plato does not claim literally to give us knowledge by means of his dialogues. In fact, he specifically denies that he has this power. He writes only to incite our minds to seek further, and perhaps he gives an inquiring mind some focus or direction in this process. The Zen master presents a problem to the novice in order to force an interiorization of thought, just because the Koan cannot be immediately solved on its surface. In fact, taken literally it makes no sense. Plato's technique admittedly is not quite so extreme. Yet fascinatingly, it has a very similar intent: to throw the listener back on self-reliance, to force one's thought to seek a deeper level. But the aim is never simply to cut off all thought.

If we say that the resulting inner experience of these nondirect techniques cannot be communicated by ordinary thought, we are only driven on to ask: is thinking of one kind only and are words only of one level of use? If "ordinary" thought is often inadequate, as many philosophers agree, can thought itself eventually be raised to greater powers? Here we come up against the question of the various modes of verbal form. We have mentioned Platonic dialogue, but the Hasidic masters preferred a story to any straightforward discourse. It may be that Elie Wiesel's dramatic narratives portray the human dilemma more profoundly than prose. Or one thinks of Blake's subtle metaphysics in verse form and the New Testament preference for parable. We must not hastily condemn all thought and language, until we can test what hidden powers they may latently possess. We must first determine in which form words are the most revelatory and the least distorting—even if they are never wholly true in any fixed form.

There may be nonliteral means of communication. If mysticism requires us to admit only that much, and if it uses strong means to point this out, then others who support reason's powers may still agree. Many positivistically oriented philosophers would not, but there is no reason to abandon reason entirely because some define it too narrowly. Neither is there any need to dismiss language because some are blind to its latent powers, those which must be excited to be realized. For John of the Cross the "dark night" leads to perfect union with God, but it is interesting to note that such an elaborate road as he describes is fully portrayable in words. Of course, there is a poetic and a symbolic element in his expression which is both heavy and essential.

John first had to purify the sensory part of the soul as well as the spiritual part, and, once this was done, a dark night descended. The soul must learn not to become attached to its visible instruments. To prevent this—very much like Descartes' method of total doubt—it works to cut itself off from all it formerly depended on. Yet John is convinced that, though the means resorted to are drastic, "once the sensory part is reformed through the purgation of the dark night, it no longer has these infirmities."[6] This statement brings us to the crucial issue: does the mystic or the Zen master induce a dark night so that perception and thought can be purified, or are they finally to be eliminated? John of course feels that each of us must pass through this crisis for ourselves. It cannot be adequately described in advance. Still, this fact can itself be stated in words.

One issue centers on the goal of union, that is, whether the soul actually can unite with God and should actively seek this. Where full union is achieved, as Plotinus has taught us, there probably is an end to all thought. But we must ask first whether union is or ought to be our goal? Is God such that he always remains distinct from other souls? If so, they still require reason and language as instruments of communication due to their distance from one another. Obscurities may persist. Reality may not be perfectly translatable into any medium. Nevertheless, if knower and known remain ultimately distinct selves, some medium of communication is still necessary. True, John feels that any attachment to creatures "defiles the soul" (p. 92), but that itself is an issue, and in any case it need not remain true always. The rational part of the soul may first have to be stilled, but is this only done as a means to bring it to greater rational power?

"Faith," St. John is convinced, "lies beyond all this understanding, taste, feeling and imagining" (p. 113) because God's being cannot be grasped by the intellect. But that raises the central question: what is God's nature like, and how, in the light of this, is he best understood? Is God like or unlike creatures in any way? If totally unlike, then reasoning will seem to be of little avail. But if God bears any identity to man, e.g., as a self, then no matter how much it may need improvement reasoning has a better chance of perfecting itself as a suitable vehicle. When we try to explain an expression used about God, e.g., that he loves the world, the explanation usually contains less than what it is embodied in the first expression. However, that need deny neither language's ability to convey nor reason's power to grasp. It may simply point to the inexhaustible levels of meaning present.

Thus, we can admit that man needs to undergo spiritual exercises, that reason needs chastisement, perhaps even the purging of its pride that plunges it into a "dark night." Still, the questions of our theory of knowledge remain. Reason is not ruled out, any more than language is as a vehicle, whatever their common abuses may be. If ultimately no "dark night" permanently characterizes the divine nature—and that is our chief point of contention with Meister Eckhart—then any purging of the mind or challenge to language is not so much ultimate as a matter of the tactics of approach. Our necessary "dark night" tells us not so much what reality is like as what human nature must be willing to go through in order to increase its power over thought. Then we move on to acquire a mastery over words as the vehicle for expressing such experience and conveying purified thought.

B. The New Rule

In an attempt to find "love beyond pain," many turn to religion. But first each must learn that no such prize is easily won. We all have to find a "new rule" for our lives and acquire a discipline that comes only at the cost of personal effort and sacrifice. Something in our life-pattern must be changed; otherwise neither can pain be stopped nor love flow freely. The rules that can be followed to achieve this are as many as the world's religions. Often these paths offered to us define how each religion differs from the others and what each can give us at what price. The practice of Yoga and Zen meditation tells us as much about their doctrine, if we listen, as do theological explanations. We learn most about a religion by watching what its practitioners do. We must observe what is required of them and how they are trained to accomplish this.

Christianity has developed its own contemplative practices and various disciplines for mystical striving. This has resulted in no single method or rule, because, we have argued, the mystical veil is temporary and for Christianity not ultimate in the nature of things. The transformation that Christianity seeks to induce in us is one that does not remove its believers from the world but transforms them in the world. The aim is to expand their ability to love. It accomplishes this by directing the emotional life away from self-concentration and toward a work that ministers to the needs of others. Christians preach a daily gospel to themselves in order to renew their spirit. They speak to others in order to explain to them the offer they carry of release to a life of love beyond pain.

Every religion involves some spiritual exercise, even if it is so calm and easily overlooked as the silence of a Quaker meeting. Every religion must involve a theology of experience too. This means that its doctrines will spread no further than the libraries of a few intellectuals unless both its preached word and its practice touch the lives of large numbers and alter their experience in desired ways. A religion can at first attract people to it simply by offering hope, but it must go beyond that to bear its "first fruits" in practice if it is to sustain its following long. In the case of Christianity, this result often comes in the form of a revolution of love. Emotion is so transformed that it is released to move beyond pain. It can now direct itself and commit itself freely (without a return demand) to needs other than the ego's own wishes.

A few "sunny religions" offer this new life at any easy price. Although momentarily attractive, such easy ways either eventually are matured in pain or else they lose their power as soon as an unfavorable wind blows. Thus, although following some set of strict rules of ascetic practice will always be for the few rather than the many, both the monk in his cell and the practitioner of Zen sitting in long hours of meditation indicate how arduous the task of release is. Christianity does have its important doctrine of grace. This says that spiritual fulfillment and release come, when they do, as a gift rather than as directly proportional to the rigor of the discipline achieved. This fact changes the Christian's relationship to all spiritual rules of prescribed practice. They become exploratory steps one must take, but they are not self-fulfilling.

The "dark night" is still a necessary stage through which each religious pilgrim must pass, but it comes about as much through personal despondency as from intensive and cultivated effort such as John of the Cross prescribes. In fact, there may be certain dangers involved in trying to self-induce such a state of emptiness, since the intensity of effort and the rigor of prescribed routine stand in contrast to the freedom and the ease with which the Christian God grants release irrespective of merit.

If ultimately release is a gift, it can be acquired as the end result of no routine. True, the ascetic in the desert may receive it, and he may have gone through strict discipline in the process. But the plumber engaged in his daily practice, no matter how sordid the level of his activities, is an equal candidate if only his emotional disposition is rightly set. If this is true, what is the place of any rule of spiritual discipline in Christian practice, and what "new rule," if developed, can hope to be effective?

These questions revolve around "spiritual transformation," how it is accomplished, and whether it can be self-defeating if directly sought after. In trying to answer this question, we are caught in the dilemma of knowing that a new state cannot even be recognized unless it is sought, while still knowing that the results achieved are not always directly proportional to the effort. Some who try hard for years will fail, insofar as their natural life span is concerned, while others who follow no such strict discipline or extreme sacrifice may be "gifted with the spirit." Transformation can be directly sought, but evidently it is not directly given—at least in the Christian understanding of God's essential freedom of action.

Almost every written rule, e.g., Saint Benedict's, involves the initial requirement of the individual's submission to authority. This is not unusual but common. In order to accept a spiritual master, one admits the need of a guide and follows an accomplished leader. All we differ over is where such authority resides, how it is conveyed, and who the master is to whom one should willingly submit. As one finds answers to these questions, one defines his or her religion. The Christian says that God is the authority and that Jesus is the Master to whom one submits. But even within that area of family agreement, there are still differences among Christians in defining how God administers his authority, what his rules are, and what exactly it means to accept Jesus as one's master.

Humanity's problem with God is at issue here. Just to the extent that one comes to discern God's nature, or the nature of ultimate reality if that person is not a theist, one understands what this God's requirements are. The issue of the efficacy of a tightly prescribed routine is in question here too. If Jesus is the master, it is the "routine" of his life that should become our pattern. All religions require the following of some prescribed routine. The only issue is how rigid this schedule is, what form it takes, and whether any human masters are accepted as its local authority. Also, one further question is involved: can this be gone about individually or does it require community effort, so that one must first seek the fellowship of a group or else fail?

The question of community vs. individual action also raises the problem of universalism. Is the transformation which any religion offers its followers available only to those who are accepted into that community and who are successful in its prescribed routines? Is the doctrine exoteric or esoteric? That is, is it offered to mankind as a whole without imposing demands that many are not equipped to meet or is it reserved for the few initiates? On this issue Christianity is rather clear. One of its earliest and most decisive inner battles, which was finally made normative in its scriptures, raged over the question of requiring all converts to conform to the Mosaic law. If enforced, this would have narrowed the offer of Christianity. The early decision recounted in Acts was not to restrict its transforming powers to any one rigid ecclesiastical practice. However, in each day the expansiveness of this offer must once again be won away from those who would restrict the offer of the Christian gospel to some set of requirements which they alone feel qualified to administer.

Again, we can see this question focused in the issue of prayer vs. meditation and what rule we must follow for each. There is no evidence that Jesus instructed his followers in any strict meditative practices, although nowhere are such rigors ruled out if found to be helpful. Jesus does pray, and he does leave his disciples instructions to pray. Yet his inclination seems to be against ritual and prescribed prayer. Again, this is not an absolute restriction, but it applies only if the discipline becomes self-seeking by its intense self-concentration, or if it becomes so oppressive a routine that it blocks the transformation of love. Prayer and meditation are not ends in themselves but rather are to be evaluated by how effectively they release one to greater human service.

In considering the desirability of any new rule for spiritual release, one must first face the problem of human sin, guilt, or wrong. It is quite clear in Christian teaching that one cannot expect improvement or make any spiritual advance without facing the question of one's own guilt. This involves wrong action toward man or God by failure to exhibit love as one should. Achieving faith is not our first problem. The question of spiritual discipline and the "new rule," the observance of which gains release—all this begins with the problem of how reparation is made for accumulated wrong and how release from one's acquired burden of guilt is secured. Of course, there are those who feel no need to repair their wrongs, and thus they fail to see that any release is needed. Such happy—or blind, as the case may be—secular, innocent people are not religiously receptive, at least at that time. Nor are they likely to seek or to accept any discipline other than their present successful—or stumbling—ways.

A turning of direction, or a desire to turn, is the initial requirement that we cannot force upon another human being. It is a move that only the individual can make. True, Christian preaching is enjoined upon all followers. Oral proclamation is designed to try to stir up the desire for personal reform, and all religions proclaim this necessity to reform nature's ways. Furthermore, our greatest urge toward our own personal confession stems from the radically transformed action of those who are newly reborn. Their testimony is shown in the way they evidence their love for one another and, more importantly, for those not a part of their group. Their nonnatural love-direction should by its example induce others to compare their lives with it, and thus perhaps come to desire a similar change.

If we want to examine the use of a tightly prescribed routine as a means to spiritual release, Ignatius of Loyola offers us his well-known example.[7] His "exercises" developed out of his own retreat. Thus, the subsequent experience of the individual who follows this prescribed way is the only test for the rightness of his outlined path. But the aim is to rid the soul of "inordinate affections" (p. 4). This raises the question of whether our goal should be so much to rid the soul of affection as to transform the directional flow of love and release it to greater effec-

tiveness. How the goal is presented has much to do with how
the steps to it are designed. Knowledge, in the philosophical
sense, is not a requirement, Ignatius is convinced (p. 7). This indicates that our attention should be given to the affections more
than to the intellect.

Gaining control over human will is the decisive factor. In
this case, spiritual discipline makes more sense as a requirement
than it does if the goal is greater understanding (p. 9). The function of solitude, vs. discourse and dialogue, is important too.
Human reason seeks company simply as a means to escape
granting greater decisive powers to the will, whereas living
in solitude places the burden more squarely on the will than the
intellect. Ignatius thinks it necessary to become "indifferent to
all created things" (p. 126). However, the question is whether it
is so much a matter of "indifference" or whether a changed attitude is the aim. Pain and punishment of the flesh are recommended, but we should first ask what is it that will most effectively produce a change of heart.

Although capable of individual variation, Ignatius prescribes a very exact and explicit order and form for the day's
routine. Our question at this point concerns the "descent of the
dove." When the Holy Spirit does enter and change a life, is its
effect anticipated and prepared for by such a life of rigor?
A rigid schedule may work well for some, but it may actually
inhibit others. If one's desire is to save one's soul (p. 129),
strictness may be required. If the aim of the rule is to produce
a change in the structure of the affections, then perhaps the
Holy Spirit may operate on a less tight schedule. The second
half of the Great Commandment is not to seek the salvation
of one's soul but to love one's neighbor. In a Christian context,
the two may amount to the same thing. But if salvation
comes only through a switch to outer-directed love, then we
must be careful about how strictly we channel our attention
toward an inward direction. To do so might work against our
eventual goal.

Humility, of course, is the aim of all spiritual exercise. To
the degree that individual confession and repentance are
prerequisite to this, the inculcation of humility as a virtue, vs.

natural pride, does require strenuous effort, unless circum-
stances conspire to destroy one's pride naturally. Effort and
direct action are no doubt involved in inducing humility. Yet if
in fact this is not a virtue that can be achieved by intensive effort, any new rule will have to be cautious about constructing
specific directions to achieve humility. As every spiritual director knows, concentration on humility itself easily becomes spiritual pride. It may be that humility is not best achieved by direct
effort but comes only as a by-product of the change in love's direction.

In attempting to define *The Essense of Zen Buddhism*,[8]
D. T. Suzuki remarks on the importance of prayer: "Prayer
opens the way to the spiritual life and finally places us in the
domain where Karma is no-Karma and no-Karma is Karma"
(p. 32). It is interesting to note that a Christian can say some,
but not all, of this too. As we learn its practice, the importance
of prayer on the development of spiritual life is clear. Yet it
cannot be said literally that prayer places the Christian in the
spiritual domain sought. Prayer alone, no matter how well
trained, simply does not have that power. The prayer may be an
appeal for guidance, and it may be necessary as preparation and
as a preliminary to our change of attitude. Nevertheless, all
conversion is the result of an infusion of the power of the Holy
Spirit from without.

Hasidism discovered the mysteries of prayer, and this carried over into the mysteries of Kabbalism.[9] The issue involved
concerns "the power of the word" vs. the preparation for
change within the soul. If one is convinced of a magic power inherent in words, then one will give painstaking loyalty to the
fixed term and to the multitude of esoteric meanings derivable
from it. Here again Christianity admits the power of the word
in some basic sense. It does not seek to abandon all verbal
power but rather to explore it. Yet, the word is simply one evidence for the spirit, a way of giving testimony to its presence.
The movement of the spirit is self-controlled and it contains all
power. The words of prayer are not themselves efficacious.
They are simply one way to prepare for the hoped-for change
which is produced only by the spirit's descent.

There is an individual redemption promised in Christianity, but on the whole this is connected to the acceptance of Jesus as the expected Messiah. That is, he comes as a phenomenon concerned with and happening to the whole body of a community. This is why any extreme individualistic searching or exclusively self-oriented ritual strikes at the heart of Christian belief. Any resulting transformation occurs to the group in virtue of their acceptance of the Messiah's presence. Thus it comes to the individual, not alone, but insofar as one makes oneself a part of a community which joins to receive that gift. Messianic redemption can only be wrought by God, and thus it defies human effort. It cannot be the result of individual meditative practice no matter how stringent or sincere.

In considering how we might institute a "new rule," we return to the question of the origin of sin and how reparation for wrongdoing is to be made and release secured. If the teachings of the Buddha say: "Each man must carry his own burden of sin and must go alone in its retribution,"[10] then the rule which each must follow will be very different, a lonely and an internal path. However, the Christian belief in the function of Jesus as savior indicates that the road is not to be traveled alone. Indeed the necessary actions to secure release have already been performed, and now they need only be shared in by the individual. One's act of sharing, of course, is itself the "new rule." This involves the new direction of love away from one's own concerns and toward the relief of suffering.

Saint Benedict proposed a "new rule" in the early sixth century. It provided a stable code for Christian community life then, and it still has amazing effectiveness today.[11] All monasticism, like Protestantism, looks back to the Apostolic Church as the source for its way of life. Thus, any "new rule" must involve a fresh capture of the first rule that governed the disciples' deportment after Jesus' removal. We know that strict moral codes and rigorous discipline were followed then, even though no single pattern reigned supreme. Nevertheless, the attempt to live strictly is a necessity. Neither the body nor the mind can be allowed free reign to gratify desire. A hedonistic age such as ours is antispiritual, except as it may induce rebellion against its own looseness. Spiritual life seems born from, although it is never identical with, some asceticism of practice. The exact form of denial, however, is left unspecified. The spirit often seems to be reborn after a society has worked hard to throw off all or most of its ethical restrictions. Then individuals or groups may rebel again, because they seek a life of greater purity for themselves once the life of sense-gratification dulls.

One withdraws from a profligate society in order to meet an inner need for discipline. Such a society does not demand this discipline, and in its permissive ways it actually inhibits any life of rigor by ridicule. The word "martyr," we need to remember and to remind Kierkegaard, does not necessarily mean one who dies. It refers simply to anyone who leads a truly self-sacrificing life. Thus, the goal of ascetic practice is primarily to encourage sacrifice for others. Lest it go wrong and turn into a masochistic love of punishment, this necessary outer direction and the root reason for discipline should not be forgotten. However, if Saint Benedict intended his rule for those who had retired from the world to work for their own salvation, as we consider forming a "new rule" for our days we should raise the question of discipline and ascetic sacrifice. Is or should the "new rule's" intention be to achieve a martyr's sacrifice to meet human need other than one's own?

Saint Benedict reports that his rule is valid only for those intending to renounce their own will (p. 291), and we must recognize this as a condition for accepting any discipline. If we are satisfied with our own performance, we feel no need to change. It is only as some acquired discipline becomes a means to self-transformation that any rigorous rule will be accepted. Thus, anyone not desiring this cannot be expected simply to accept some existing external authority, whether religious or political. Benedict clearly recognizes that words are not enough. One may teach a law of conduct by verbal instruction, but the only really effective means to demonstrate that one has learned from another is by the example of actually living in the newly prescribed manner. The rule must be seen embodied in conduct to be believed. Of course, Benedict primarily has in mind the procedural rules for governing a community of monks, and he does assume that the seclusion of the monastery is the best place for such practice to be carried out (p. 299). Therefore, our question becomes: how can an altered life-style be achieved without withdrawal from society but rather within its midst?

Humility and obedience are the keys to any success in finding new ways of life (pp. 300-304), Benedict informs us. But we must ask: in what ways can one be obedient to God, and what can induce the humility necessary before inner change is possible? To "obey" God is said to mean to love and to serve one's neighbor in need, but we must first come to decide what God is like before such a desire can become pressing for us. Accompanying this we need a genuine humility about our own accomplishments. It may be that the proud can never see God. They cannot therefore discover his "new rule" until they accept the fact that, in spite of their own accomplishments, no fundamental change in human nature can be brought about from their effort alone. A prior conversion of direction and a new attitude are required. Once we feel the urge to change, we can make the proposal and confess this need, but all effective change and release must still come to us as a gift.

Notes to Chapter III

1. *The Teachings of the Buddha* (Federation of Young Buddhist Associations), p. 109.

2. D. T. Suzuki, *Mysticism: Christian and Buddhist* (London: George Allen and Unwin, 1937), p. 48.

3. Bernard Phillips, Ed., *The Essentials of Zen Buddhism* (Westport, Conn.: Greenwood Press, 1973), p. 32.

4. *The Teachings of the Buddha, op. cit.*, p. 75.

5. Georg Hegel, *Phenomenology of Mind*, trans. J. B. Baillie (New York: Harper and Row, 1967), p. 70.

6. *The Collected Works of St. John of the Cross*, trans. K. Kavanaugh and O. Rodriguez (London: Nelson, 1964), p. 304. All page references are to this edition.

7. Ignatius of Loyola, *Spiritual Exercises*, trans. W. H.

Longridge (London: A. R. Mowbray, 1955).

8. D. T. Suzuki, *The Essence of Zen Buddhism* (Kyoto, Hozokan, 1968).

9. See Gersholm G. Scholem, *Major Trends in Jewish Mysticism* (New York: Schocken Books, 1961), pp. 101-102.

10. *The Teachings of the Buddha, op. cit.*, p. 90.

11. "The Rule of Saint Benedict," in *Western Asceticism*, trans. Owen Chadwick (London: SCM Press, 1958).

IV

An Instrument of Peace

A. Man Becoming God

Much of the spiritual direction offered, as well as the discipline advised to implement it, has the explicit intention of enabling man to become God, or at least God-like. The Way of Purification in the *Teachings of Buddha*[1] advocates "mind control" as the means to this goal. Partly this path involves withdrawal from society, but the issue remains: can one remain with and live among evil men and still seek transformation? Strict control will of course be necessary, as is the selective purging of desire, but the question becomes: how powerful can the mind be in accomplishing this self-transformation? Is the mind the master, and does it have the power to make desire disappear (p. 109)? This is not so much a skeptical question that attempts to downgrade the mind's powers. It only opposes a "high mentalism." That is, it questions whether we should place primary confidence in the mind's self-transforming powers.

What can we hope to accomplish by "mind control," we need to ask. First of all, we know that no large group can be uniformly transformed, only special individuals. Once again, we are led to the priority of the question of God's nature. What is God like? Is he content with a few who achieve wisdom and virtue? If not, it would seem that more is required than the tight discipline that some are able to sustain, even if such a strict path has the effect of altering a few substantially. Is our goal to achieve a union with God and a blissful state of contemplation, or is the primary issue to try to see what God is like? How can we know God more fully, and what does the God we discover seem to require of us? If there were only one God for us to encounter, or only one agreed spiritual goal, the prior question of how to discern God's will would not be so important, but we are

50

faced with plural Gods and plural ways.

We know that no one begins life with full knowledge of God, so our question becomes: how and by what means do we come to know God more fully? In the light of our answer, we want to know what transformations can take place, and how would such a God advise that we accomplish this task? What does this God, or that picture of Reality, require of us, and how is the needed transformation to be accomplished? The often professed desire to "become one with God" really transforms itself into the question of what unity with that God would be like, and our versions of such a state can vary. If God's nature, for instance, requires that we become instruments of peace, the goal of union really means how our powers can be used so that our effective peaceful instrumentality is increased.

All spirituality is mystical in its realization that the laws of logic and of nature must be transcended, if we are to be renewed and if our power to accomplish regeneration is to be increased. The issue is, how can such a transcendence of our present restrictions take place, and is it available for many or for the few only? Surely we must begin our answer by admitting that humankind and God both possess some individual power in this matter. However, this does not solve the question of the scope of each and the desired balance to be achieved in the exercise of these powers. The needed process is one of transformation, but does that involve a loss of self, or is the self something substantial that can be preserved essentially but still transformed in the process?

Now we encounter the question of God's own mysticism. Is God himself a self, rather than the absence of all such structures —whether this emptiness comes about by transcendence or otherwise? Does every mystical way seek self-transcendence, or can our goal simply be the transformation of the self into a more pure and responsive form? If so, the self is not an illusion to be abandoned, but rather it is an acceptable core, one not too unlike the divine center. Our human self requires reformation, not abolition. If the religious individual vs. the secular wants to become God, we must first determine what God is like before we can decide how far our powers extend to accomplish this.

What means must we use, and will the result still be a self or something beyond that?

Our answer to the question of how and whether humankind becomes God, and what the result of such a quest is, will depend on what mysticism means. If it means to "identify with God," the loss of the individual self is required, and the overcoming of all separation of selves is a necessity. Is logical consistency ultimate, or is rationality a human impediment not characteristic of God's nature and thus something for humanity to overcome too? What is the function of that which cannot be fathomed, e.g., a Zen Koan? Is it only a means to block the intellect from its tendency to take too simple a route, to accept some self-consistent theory as a real answer? Or is our aim to drive the mind into reflection and to mature its sensitivities to what lies beyond easy grasp? If it is the latter, nothing is beyond ultimate apprehension, although we may set up blocks to the mind's normal operation in order to force it to achieve what it could not if we left the mind confident and unopposed.

How ultimate is logical consistency? Are God's mind and his operations bound by it too, or is this a limitation of lesser minds and thus a block to our self-transformation? Is the mind that discriminates not the true mind?[2] If this is the case, logical consistency will have to be overcome. On the other hand, we can admit that often our minds are unable to escape their self-imposed confines so long as other avenues of thought remain open, and this is the main obstacle to improvement. Still, we can insist that the discriminating function is true mind. The mind we know simply needs expansion rather than elimination. Logic may have more forms than one. If so, then within its limit lies all the flexibility we need, if we can first understand the vastness and variability of God's consistency vs. our own.

Might mysticism mean not humankind's becoming God through union with him but the experience of charismatic gifts? The gifts of the spirit transport one outside the self. If so, the issue is not one of overcoming the self in divine union. Everything depends on the adoption of some kind of discipline that can lead to transcendence. Kabbalism may use the magic of alphabet, name and number, but this need not prove God's supra-rationality. It speaks more of our dependence on a certain discipline and of our need for a training that forces us to detach the mind's tight grip in order to open our too-restricted reception. Spiritual gifts cannot come to all without some force of entry. People must first prepare themselves. But if techniques become an end in themselves and not a means, they actually distort reality and block the Holy Spirit's descent, no matter how desirable they are in the abstract.

The function and value of that which cannot be fathomed is that it brings thought temporarily to a stop. It turns the person inward because he or she can no longer move forward easily. Suzuki takes the position that logical consistency is not ultimate,[3] and this assertion does bring up the crucial issue. Yes, we want to stop the intellect's clever dodges that protect the self from the very exposure that might move it to seek a cure. Logical consistency might still govern God's thought, although he is surely capable of greater range and subtlety than our usual use of logic involves. We limit ourselves too rigidly, but there is no need to deny all limit to God for that reason. The issue may be one of a self-imposed limit vs. a restriction placed on us from outside. We restrict ourselves and are restricted by others, and thus we need to develop a will to bring thought to a stop so that it can seek its own release.

The writings of the Hasidic masters are full of epigram and aphorism. Does this show a disregard for logical consistency, or does it rather reflect a primary need to expand the mind's grasp by the use of indirect techniques? The story form makes Kabbalism available to masses of people, when otherwise it would be confined to an esoteric minority. Individual redemption can be achieved by individual extreme action, but the transformation of the mass or the whole body of a community can be accomplished by God alone. Literature and ritual practice do not embody Hasidic achievement, no matter how well they are learned. They merely promote the preparation for a change that must be introduced from outside. Thus, the only person we need is the changed one. One whose heart has been touched and remade by God is the spark that can ignite the fire in us.

The charisma, the gift of revival, stems not from our individual efforts but from outside us, however far our own struggles go toward preparing us to receive it. Personality here takes the place of doctrine, for it is not so much a matter of following a teacher of the correct word as it is of identifying with a model whose very actions are inspired. It is not the model's abstract knowledge but his or her life that counts. And if personality takes the place of doctrine in this way, it is hard to see how selfhood can ever be eliminated in God. Perhaps God uses inspired selves as instruments of transformation, even in preference to issuing correct doctrine. Therefore, the self is not the main obstacle blocking individual regeneration. It only stands in need of a new infused spirit.

If direct, spontaneous religious experience is the medium of transforming power, then everything becomes a story of these works, not simply a theory as such. The Hasid avoids elaborate theoretical discussion too, much as the Zen master does. This is not because mind and self must be finally set aside, but because the spirit-filled individual is our source of release. Spiritual power is best portrayed and conveyed by story rather than by doctrine or the ascetic suppression of intellect. The tale, the account of charismatic deeds, these of course retain a mysticism of their own just because they are not reducible to one formula. The search for a unity of theory is the prime criterion the mind uses in its discriminating function. Intellect is not, however, set aside by denying this goal. It is only infused with greater power by the inspired self.

"To come back to oneself in an instant: that is what awakening consists in," says the famous Chinese Zen Text, *The Ox and His Herdsman*.[4] Thus, the fundamental question is not the overcoming of self, not our union with God nor the elimination of logic nor the discriminating qualities of the mind. Ours is, rather, a practical question: what can disengage the self from absorption with its own ego demands? What can distance the self from itself and drive it into interior inspection? When this can be done, the self can be led out again to receive reconstituted power. This may take place via any one of the offered mystical ways, the Zen experience of emptiness, Plotinus' path to union with the One, or John of the Cross's plunge into a "dark night." If the Kabbalistic way or Hasidic story or a Zen Koan accomplishes the redirection of the self, fine. It is a matter of which technique is efficacious rather than the absolute rightness of any given doctrine—a conclusion not far from what the Zen master hopes to communicate by harsh means.

The gift of what the soul needs comes only in a nonliteral mode. Here is the limit of philosophy. Concentration on the literalness of verbal form has been one cause of the self's restriction and failure in its tightness, but this is not because the discreteness of logical distinction is absolutely false. The mind needs to be released from its tendency to treat verbal form as absolute and as capable of containing truth as such. Some techniques for accomplishing this are more radical than others, e.g., Zen meditation under a strict master. But all aim at the release of the soul from a slavery to words. The rejection of logic seems extreme at times, but words are so obvious and handy that a weak mind falls back on them too easily. The self must be radically weaned from its natural tendency to an unexamined dependence on the process of thought held in isolation from emotion and will.

Once it has achieved detachment, can the self then become more open to receive an inspired spirit and still return to use words in human communication more cautiously and also more powerfully? Few will ever abandon speech and writing totally. What is involved is a matter of our degree of dependence and the use of varied forms of approach to words. The Zen Koan is as verbal in its presentation as the Hasidic tale. Yet both are, hopefully, of such a nature as to force the receiving mind to greater depths of self-understanding. The aim is to induce skill in the use of symbols, whether verbal or otherwise. Zen stresses, quite subtly and quite rightly, that the attachment to any means or achieved state, as if it were in itself absolute, is a perversion of the aim of release. The rigid Wittgensteinian mocks the master, just as a scholarly treatment of Kierkegaard does. Thus, we begin with freedom in our choice of the method we use to open the soul, both for its initial transformation and then for its release from all dogmatism of final conclusion.

A free self is a free self is a free self, however it is achieved.

The given manual or rule that you like may lead another effectively, and again it may not. The inspiration of a charismatic figure is more important than is any absolute certainty of technique, although words become efficacious when the teacher is located behind them, whether this teacher is contemporary or ancient. The mind seeks healing where it can find it. But if the result is an absolute fixity to one method, this is the most telling denial of the spirit's hoped-for final freedom, since then it has simply become addicted to its medicine. Much depends on the vision of God or Reality as it is given to the individual. Thus, if Zen doctrine does not match your disclosure of Reality, it is useless. If, however, the technique used is designed precisely to release the individual for one's own disclosure of Reality or God —or to let God or Reality disclose itself—then the details of the method are unimportant. They can be set aside and not absolutized once Reality is apprehended and the soul is released to new power.

However, no passage to freedom and new life is without that precarious and crucial moment when loss is as possible as gain. Modern science hoped to find a single foolproof methodology for use in every area of life. Whether such singularity holds for the physical sciences or not, it is certain that the reconstruction of the individual self can never take place by a guaranteed process. The Zen text on "*The Ox and His Herdsman*"[5] speaks of the oblivion of doubt and confusion (p. 33). Like John of the Cross, Descartes subjects the mind to total doubt, but what Descartes never doubts is his assured outcome. In radical learning, why are the dark night of the senses and the peril of loss such crucial experiences? Like the frustration of reason, the self cannot receive charismatic gifts as long as it hides in safety. How can we be made to venture? The passage through a "dark night" purifies us in a way no method of certainty could hope to. The self must be disengaged from its stable ties if it is to become free. Security, however comfortable, is not freedom.

The teachings of the Buddha tell us that the ego soul must be "abandoned" if one is to realize enlightenment, but we must scrutinize this statement carefully. Must the ego be let go in the passage through a "dark night," if it is ever to be given back to us free and with renewed power? Or, is the loss of ego an absolute one? It could go either way. Our answer depends on whether the soul is thought of as at first perfect and divine and only later acquires that which corrupts it. If so, the goal is to recover this lost pure state. But if the soul has never been that perfect, our desired transformation is one that moves away from our basic nature. It is not just the recovery of something once rightfully possessed. If radical alteration is required, the self is not by nature divine, but still it might be raised to that level by an infused spirit.

When so transformed, does the self remain a self, or does it lose itself in something beyond such confines? If the ego-self is only abandoned temporarily and not ultimately, our theory of knowledge need not seek for a truth beyond the mind's grasp of categories and its need to rely on distinctions. If our knowing apparatus never was without flaw, the degree of success now possible is not the recovery of some lost purity. Release depends on a reformation of the self that makes it a more adequate receiving instrument and a more enlightened bearer and user of truth. We seek a state we have never known, something we cannot claim once rightfully belonged to us. We reach for powers not naturally bestowed on all, even if they are potential to everyone. The transformation we seek is not primarily an intellectual affair.

The question turns on discovering how one can become an instrument of peace. If we see God's nature as embodying this aim, and the Christian does, the issue is how one can increase peace and not war, life and not destruction. Jesus says "Behold I stand at the door and knock, and if any man will open the door, I will come in." This image defines the role of God and the role of humanity. The transformation can be forced from outside, but it seldom is. The spring of release lies in an inner opening, which leads us at first to a "dark night" as much as to anything else. But the setting aside of self which is involved is neither necessary nor final. The enforced loss is a means to achieve release from attachment to that which hinders any infusion of charismatic spirit and enhanced powers.

Every technique or rule or way of transformation must

have a goal. The religions of the world would all be one, instead
of at odds with one another, if the goal of each were the same.
"Enlightenment," "union with God," a "reborn self," "freedom
from sin and guilt"—all these and more formulate the various
religious ways. Each reflects how God or Reality is seen, and
each doctrine involves an appropriate way or technique for
achieving this desired end. For some, human beings become
God or return to a divine state. For others, humanity transforms humanity. God fades when religious ferver grows cold,
and we become skeptical about any technique or discipline because we question or doubt the proposed goal. Sometimes this is
due to the fact that we have lost a vision of God as himself
being like our ideal. If we are not sure he sits in Buddha-like
meditation, sometimes it is because we vaguely discern another
goal and state we prefer for both God and the human self.

The search for transformation must be preceded by the
desire to have a re-formed self, and this must be tied to a vision
of God or Power which by nature is like that state, one capable
of effecting or assisting in the transformation. If so, what would
the acceptance of the goal of becoming "an instrument of
peace" involve, and what discoveries might this lead to? First,
we see that the issue at hand becomes a question of "belief"
only in the sense of whether one accepts that goal for life or not.
It is not a matter of being asked to accept elaborate doctrinal
propositions. Theologies may be developed out of the goal, of
course, but the aim must be accepted before the propositions
have validity. Also, the chief test for truth is one of altered
human behavior, not doctrinal conformity by the intellect.

As naturally born, people sometimes are instruments of
peace, but this idyllic situation is all too seldom true. A state of
nature is a state of war, as politicians know better than philosophers. We perhaps yearn for peace naturally, but our own
aggressive and protective tendencies act against this, unless the
instinct to satisfy desire can be not controlled but transformed.
God cannot be without his warrior side, since religion and political power have so often been allied. People have and still do go
to war and kill in the name of religion. God must bear some
relationship to and responsibility for both the world's destruc-

tive bent and humanity's self-frustrating passions. But if we come to see God as an instrument of peace, which we too would like to be altered to become, our revelation of God becomes one of a balance of forces. There must be an inner and a sometimes hidden self in the divine nature, one in which peace emerges as the dominant factor although it is not normally disclosed.

Except in a few specially endowed souls, human nature exhibits no such peaceful balance at present. And even those whose lives exemplify peace seldom possess the power of control exercised by those who are of more aggressive and less peaceful inclinations. The meek may inherit what is left of the world, but they do not rule it now. The Garden of Eden is more the symbol of a desired state than it is a historical description of what human beings once were like. The law of survival of the fittest and of evolution from lower species more accurately explain humanity as we find it. Yet we feel a desire to become clearer in our vision of how God is able to deal effectively with so much greater passion, desire, and destruction than we can even know. How can any self become a center for overcoming strife? Can we become instruments of a peace which other selves are then reborn to share in too?

B. *The Transformation of Love*

Love of a sentimental kind works to make one mild and sweet and accepting. The problem is that love of this kind does not make you an instrument of peace. Far from it; it is often the source of conflict. Even if the individual becomes peaceful, the destructive powers abroad in the world that need control are not subdued. Force, violence and a desire to control are necessary qualities in nature, but they are also the very factors that upset peace. Thus, the world has produced its saints, and still it knows neither inner nor outer peace except at rare moments. It takes power to rule, but we are aware of the truth of the adage that power tends to corrupt. This is why, in both politics and religion, we have so often witnessed a desperate and ruthless use of power wielded in an attempt to make others conform.

In what respects, then, is love *not* an instrument of peace? We must come to understand this before we can discover how love might be transformed to become one. We celebrate love, but, like Socrates in the *Symposium*, we are at the same time aware that we are simply praising a passion that has many forms—some good, some bad. No one who has not been gripped in the power of a passion so strong that it becomes obsessive can understand the magnitude of the problem before us. Then one is rendered helpless except to seek its continued fulfillment. Some say they are not touched by these impelling forces. They live easy lives, but neither are they the source of our human problem. So many people are driven by desires beyond their control that the human scene as a whole will know no lasting calm until these passions can be controlled or converted to a peaceful use.

Love, we know, tears at people and can destroy them as well as pit them against each other. Beautiful women and gold are both scarce commodities. We war because we desire the same prized object and only one can possess it. Exclusive desire creates antagonism, as Spinoza pointed out. He recommended that we all pursue the love of God, because that is something we all can share in equally. The problem with Spinoza's proposal is that we do not all see God alike, or even see him at all. Thus, we tend to fall into an argument over God rather than to seek him peacefully.

God is as much a cause of war as of peace, at least as he has been variously conceived or his image bent out of shape to side with certain human ambitions. Love makes us restless, as every lover who is driven to distraction knows. In point of fact, only at rare moments does love produce peace and bliss. Thus, to identify love with its ecstatic aspects both misses the full range of its powers and vastly oversimplifies the problem. If love always brought peace, novelists would all become unemployed and newspaper reporting would be much less sensational.

Love may lead us to heights of joy. More often it tends to destroy, to dominate and to disturb. The dreams of human beings are not restful precisely because love is so difficult to satisfy, as Freud discovered. A generation that has concentrated its efforts on direct and explicit satisfaction knows this just as well as a Victorian age that preached restraint, discretion and abstinence, and tolerated only a private, indirect expression of affection. Not to know love is to miss a great deal, but our loves are so many and so varied that it is foolish to pretend they are all satisfied either by sex or by what we call our love affairs. Human desires range too wide and extend to too many objects, both tangible and intangible, for that to be true. Many marriages are disturbed and broken because one partner thinks a universal and multi-faceted desire should be fulfilled in one object or expressed in a single relationship. If the love of power does not allow itself to be so concentrated in one outlet, why should any other form of love submit to unity so easily or be domesticated without a struggle?

Sometimes we think of love as an instrument of enlightenment. Plato thought it could be. But in the *Phaedrus* he correctly saw that many forms of love are not instructive. Only rarely —although importantly—is love's madness of the divine sort that reveals what has heretofore remained hidden. In a Dionysian spirit of exhaltation, we tend to exalt and to extoll all of love's excesses. We simplify life and pretend that love's induced frenzy is always beneficial. It would be better to admit that very often we are led near to a state of addiction and cannot refrain, rather than to claim enlightenment from the experience of a flood of passion. Some are raised to new heights, but most human beings are blinded and so driven or obsessed by passion that they lose both control and perspective. We often see least clearly just when we need to see most clearly, if we are to hope to escape the blindness of passion and to find peace.

Love leads some few to new heights of insight, just as Plato described it. But the rareness of this occurrence and the often destructive results of passion prevent love in its raw state from solving the human problem. Love is too seldom enlightening to be able of itself to reverse the tide of tangled human emotions that primarily are blinding in their effect. If love releases some few, it does not have the power to release many. Both Freud and Spinoza thought that reason could probe passion and produce a full understanding which then could succeed in emotion's control. However, the understanding of Spinoza is rare and not universal; Freud's detailed analysis of eros can be neither widely administered nor made effective in every case. Since neither philosophers nor psychiatrists are allowed to run the affairs of the world, however much we dream and fantasize that they might. The mass of humanity remains more subject to love's destructive force and its blindness than to its enlightening qualities. Or at least it is safe to say that we are blind if we rely on love to produce peace.

Yet where does this leave us? Should all our energy perhaps go toward achieving individual union with God? This is a rare state that leaves the emotions of most unsatisfied. In spite of its high religious motivation, it also tends to stress individual fulfillment first, just as much as if we concentrated all love into sex. The ability of one person to create techniques to satisfy either one's own religious longing or sexual desire adds to the general problem, because all of these avenues concentrate the individual in himself or herself. Thus such techniques ironically make one less able to offer oneself more generally to others. Shall we train a few in Zen meditation and certify the attainment of Satori by a small band of spiritual athletes? Some may negate their passions and achieve a neutrality that allows calm action, in archery or calligraphy or in motorcycle maintenance. Yet the waves of passion and the powers of love that break over the heads of most men and women cannot be controlled simply by calling a few in out of the storm.

Can the transformation of love be offered as a universal possibility open to all? Can love retain its power but reverse its direction by moving love from self-concentration to an outer direction? Can the destructive and blinding aspects of all ecstatic experience, drugs included, be so controlled and contained that love increases vision and heightens human power rather than locking us in to ourselves all the more? Can the desires and passions that create war and tension, vice and scandal, not be castrated into meek and impotent toys but instead be formed as powerful instruments of peace? Can love and noble desire, which so easily explode into violence and hate, be held at that borderline that achieves a fundamental change but does not self-destruct?

Most religions seek an answer to this puzzle, although all

do not do so in the same way. Some ask different questions; some find different paths and respond to new Gods. But as far as Christianity is concerned, like Thomas a Kempis its followers have always sought to achieve an *Imitation of Christ.*[6] However, the reason why Christians are not all of one political body, and why we have a history of internal persecution of one another, is that some give a primacy to matters of doctrine and ecclesiastical office. Not all Christians will agree that their goal and life are defined by the practical imitation of a lived way.

Furthermore, even if we accept our primary religious aim to be a change in life's direction, we are all still able to see Jesus in different ways. We lack a norm for reading Christian history and its founding acts in a way which of itself provides only one path. We simply blind ourselves if we claim that one offered path is the only right or acceptable way, whereas in fact we know that various ages have produced various models of Christ with varying degrees of effectiveness. If any mode captures and transforms people, it provides an acceptable goal. But new times need new or revised models. Can one be found again today?

Thomas a Kempis advises us to "conform our life as nearly as we can to His" (p. 31), but our problem is to see just what this special life was like as it was once lived. Thomas denies that reason has the ability to create the humility necessary to accomplish this conformation. He does not deny the strength of the understanding to understand, but he questions its power to redirect emotion. However, Thomas strikes the key issue when his plan for imitation recommends that we "withdraw the love of the soul from all things that are visible, and to turn it to things that are invisible" (p. 30). In the first place, it is questionable that this is what Jesus did. In the second place, even if this is true it may save the soul of the one who withdraws, but it can hardly be expected to affect the rest of the visible world very much.

Thomas advises us that the most profitable learning is to despise oneself (p. 33), but it is not clear either that Jesus did this or that he recommended it for his followers. There are human desires that must be turned around and actions that must be corrected. However, if we are to love our neighbors as ourselves, we first must come to love ourselves in a non-self-gratifying way. And it is amazing how many cannot love themselves easily but have, as Kierkegaard called it, a "sickness unto death," a wish to be rid of at least certain aspects of themselves.

Thomas is not sure that a scientific knowledge of the natural order is of much avail, but such understanding of nature can provide both a context for increased self-understanding and a control of nature, which we do need. Action is primary, and it forms the sole basis for judgment; Thomas is right (p. 35). The issue is whether all that we read and listen to and attempt to understand is simply a necessary preliminary to pave the way for action.

As a means of self-protection, Thomas wants us to open ourselves only to those who are wise, discreet and reverent. Ironically, it is not certain that Jesus himself followed this cautious path. His involvement with people seems to include more danger than such a discreet course allows, and certainly it demands a greater openness. We can flee the company of worldly persons, as Thomas recommends, but we are not likely to change or affect them very much unless we constantly take the risk of a variety of personal associations. Jesus did not restrict himself to a cell of pure piety. Quite the opposite, he did not even avoid Judas. Saints have been contemplative, and this is a universal tendency of the religious instinct, but there is little evidence that Jesus himself followed or advised this particular route. His mode of extension is more out into the world.

Still, if we are directed toward the world and for good reasons, how can we avoid being controlled by its cycle of passions? This question is what always leads to the logic of withdrawal. Thomas advises us to abandon curiosity, and he tells us that the most holy men have fled the company of worldly minded men (p. 55). That may be true, but, ironically, it does not seem to be true of Jesus. Most of the world is driven by curiosity. To avoid the human tendency to explore is simply to fail to recognize the forces operative in the natural order. Jesus did withdraw from the world, but only for the brief time of preparation for his public ministry. His normal pattern, which we are instructed to imitate, is directed to the world. He ministers to its needs by word and healing—and also by instruction and reproof when necessary. The battle that must be joined does lead toward apparent self-destruction.

Thomas thinks earthly joys are pleasant at first but that in the long run they gnaw and kill (p. 57). However, some natural joys stay quite pleasant. The issue before us is not one of avoiding them but of curbing their self-destructive tendencies. Thomas wants us to die to the world so that we may live with Christ (p. 65). However, to imitate such a life is not that simple, since to "live with Christ" is to move once again into the world, although now in a new way. Our problem is to discover how the transformation of love into a non-destructive power can take place. Our need is not to escape from all natural desire. We may be pilgrims, but we are not strangers to this world. Or, if any religion is, it will not affect the masses much. Human beings seek retribution; most pursue it covertly and with a vengeance. We are told God does not. Wonderful; but how is the widespread human vindictiveness we face to be transformed?

Thomas wants us to turn to God and "forsake this wretched world" (p. 73). Jesus turned to God, but this did not involve forsaking the world. To live in the tension that this split attention creates is the actual imitation of Christ. If we let our thoughts always be upward toward God (p. 76), they will merely come back down to us again with an added command to serve others. The issue is what kind of God we discover in our lives, and he may not be one who withdraws from the world in contemplation. Significantly, Thomas thinks that people are troubled because they are not "fully severed from the love of earthly things" (p. 78), and he is right. But such separation is not the only available cure. Instead, it is the transformation of earthly love that we seek. To stifle love is frustrating, but in a way isn't that less demanding than to learn the art of its control?

Should perfect happiness and inward peace be our central goal? Or is the struggle of humanity with the world such that it never allows full happiness, although a certain form of peace may be achieved if one abandons one's own desires and assumes the misery of others? To love Jesus is to love creatures, since that is where his own love is directed. Jesus did not despise all that is pleasurable and delectable in the world, but he did want to rid it of self-absorption and its destructive tendencies.

Thomas admonishes us to make ourselves "pleasing in His Sight" (p. 104), and we all would all like to be pleasing in the sight of those we love. The issue is how to do this and how to discover what Jesus regards as "pleasing." We know what pleases the editors of *Playboy*. Jesus is more difficult to fathom, since he does not shun the beauties in the world. Instead, he seems to work within the given human context, all the while aiming to release us from its defective forms of expression.

Perhaps we can find protection against the constant religious, and also psychological, tendency simply to reject in disgust what we have previously been associated with. But to achieve this, we must see every outer struggle, whether over wife, empire, position or approval, as simply symbolic of an inner battle. Would any of the struggles we fight on or over the earth's surface take place if we did not first battle with ourselves and then exteriorize this conflict? The problem is that most people do not recognize the origin of their struggles in this way. Thus the material prize is taken to be that which the self needs for its own sake. Since the inner struggle often goes on independently from the outer, we are disquieted when the exterior public battle is either won or lost but our interior situation does not respond in like fashion. The extreme remedy for such spiritual imbalance is to impugn and renounce all material desires. The more realistic way is to carry out the battle simultaneously on two fronts. One victory is not enough. Two are required. Each demands different talents, specially acquired disciplines, and new sensitivities.

Of course, the saddest people in the world are those who are locked into their own inner struggles. Some lack either the power or the talent to escape by redirecting their concern to someone else or to some external project. The one who can become totally absorbed in physical or material combat, even to the neglect of his or her own soul, is almost more to be admired. Surely such a person is more fun to be around, and possibly also safer to associate with. The most dangerous people are those who mistake you for their enemy, when really it is their own uncontrolled interior forces that need to be faced, but they cannot bring themselves to do so. "Render unto the inner psyche that which belongs to it and unto the material forces of the world the physical counter-force which they require."

Yet, in a Christian sense the aim is not to win battles for the sheer fun of it—not even the crucial inner spiritual battle. The goal is to wield power in such a way that love is transformed and we become effective instruments of peace. That is the way we convert ourselves to lead a life like Jesus, and that is what its "imitation" means. The imitation of Christ transforms the self by transforming love, and not by the too-simple Augustinian scheme of directing affection away from the world and toward God. Love of God is not a simple matter, because the irony of the Christian message is that God has announced that he is in love with the world. Thus, to love him is to share his love of the human. The Christian gospel also claims that God has moved and is moving to create instruments of peace. How is this done, and what can we do to share in such an important operation?

In the first place, a divine offer exists that claims to provide us with the power to change. Yet to hear the gospel and to be affected by it is not simple. Accepting its offer does not mean verbal confession or proper creedal affirmation. These come after the deed as its reflection. The test is one of altered intentions. We can seldom (not never, just seldom and then only by heroic gifts of strength and talent) transform our own love to nondestructive and enlightening vs. blinding expression. However, all may come to the declaration of a new intention. Even those who do are not immediately caught up by the divine offer, since its timing is such that any resulting transformation is seldom immediate. It may take different forms in different individuals. For this reason, faith means to have confidence in the final day of delivery, even if the initial arrival is slow in appearing. This change may be hard to discern, if we judge by the appearance of present behavior that is not altered significantly.

Furthermore, the love of God is achieved and expressed in surprising ways, not just in ecstatic union. This is not hard to understand when we realize that human love need not always be expressed primarily in sexual union. Sometimes love is clearer and more gratifying if it is not consummated physically, since such overt action can easily be confusing because it identifies a sensitive and subtle inner state with a simple physical expression. If everything one feels is immediately and directly expressed in physical form, this may lead to spiritual impoverishment and inner confusion. Many matters are better dealt with by interior means, and silently too. We need time to discover what the most trusted and least harmful form of expression might be. We may actually frustrate desire if we give it expression too quickly. And immediate satisfaction also robs desire of its ability to deepen our inward reflection. A life totally outwardly expressed risks the loss of ever discovering what self-renewal means.

God moves to create instruments of his peace by increasing a depth of love within, since shallow people know only either an embrace or a blow. If Jesus was God's embodiment for this purpose, he was an instrument of peace because he refused to yield to oppressive force. Still, he refrained from inciting the excessive violence that only destroys no matter how noble its aim. His indirection of message, the fact that he did not simply express overtly all he thought—this is his example, and it can stir a similar deepening of sensitivity and reflection in us. It induces a like-mannered caution in the use of words and acts. Simple solutions are to be shunned because love is more complex and tricky—and also more important—than economics. The fact that perpetual peace has not come to earth is not simply because economics has not yet been fully brought under control.

Thus, the material forces of the world are very real and very powerful. They induce their own loves, although probably these assume alternate forms and not just one. Love is neither parallel to reason in its motion, nor is it capable of subordination to or direct expression by reason. Nevertheless, love can be understood. It need not be transcended into an empty state which is neither love nor hate. Thus, the creation of a human instrument of peace involves prior instruction in the ways of love. We must learn how to thread our way among tangled human emotions in order to sort out those that promote peace and not combat. But first comes the surgical act by which we sever the nerve that attaches every emotion to some self-interest. This is the same cord that keeps every human effort directed back to our own enhancement. The key is to be able to achieve an unattached outward flow of emotion. Otherwise love always continues to struggle against itself.

This brings us to the issue of the loss of self, since a total absence of all self-love would seem to be equivalent to death. Ironically, we know we cannot love another person if we have ceased to love ourselves, or if we are trapped in our own mixed feelings of self-hatred. The self that merely struggles for its place in the sun eventually dies, but love purified as an instrument of peace generates rebirth. The old self is selectively restructured. Love comes to us at first entangled with destructive passions, which means that only certain forms and directions of emotion should be certified for expression.

God is constantly engaged in this selective self-transformation in order to promote peace. Modeled on his example, human beings contain within themselves the same potential for peaceful love. That is, they do if they will first undergo an elaborate selective surgery on the bundle of emotions that form the self as it is given to us and develops in the natural world. Raw love immediately expressed is self-defeating due to the conflicts it generates. Love purified by inner struggle can transform the self into an instrument of peace. It also places reason in its proper role as mediator between the intellect and what is different from itself, that is, the emotions and the will. But the act of preparation (the struggle) is different from the act of release (the descent of the spirit). One comes from the inside, the other arrives from without. One is human, and one is God's peculiar act.

Notes to Chapter IV

1. *The Teachings of Buddha, op. cit.,* p. 106.

2. Ibid., p. 69.

3. *The Essentials of Zen Buddhism, op. cit.*, p. 50.

4. *The Ox and His Herdsman*, trans. M. H. Trevor (Tokyo: The Hokuseido Press, 1969), p. 37.

5. Ibid., p. 71.

6. *Imitation of Christ*, trans. Richard Whitford, ed. Harold C. Gardner, S.J. (Garden City, N.Y.: Image Books, 1955).

V

Conversion

A. Free Expression

The conversion of the self that we desire is the one that will allow us to speak both freely and with power. Along with all philosophers, ordinary people have long sought to find a way to express themselves that will enable their thoughts to flow freely in unimpeded communication. Normally, we face barriers that prevent us from making our thoughts and feelings evident to ourselves as well as to others. It is equally hard to know the exact sentiments that sway other people. We are seldom known in the way we would like to be known, that is, granted that we are not intentionally trying to hide or engage in some elaborate cover-up. In our imagination, "God" stands for the epitome of free expression. He may hide or he may seem to be hidden now, but to our minds he represents that power capable of completely free and unfettered expression. His infinity, at least in one aspect, consists of his ability to make himself fully known whenever he wishes to.

Often we think of free expression or free speech as synonymous with the removal of all restraints. And it is true that, at least at present, we think of ourselves as inhibited in our expression by the limitations and restrictions placed on us that block our natural flow. This is true to some extent. Actually, what we need is our own conversion if communication is to be clear and direct and not simply a relief from external restraints. It is ourselves as we now are that block free expression. We need to ask: what kind of conversion of the normal self must take place in order to allow direct and unmediated communication? And how can such a "new self," one that is made fully intelligible, be brought into existence?

All education and training teaches us how to control and to

71

use our minds. To accomplish a similar release for the spirit, some religions have concentrated on the necessity of each individual's breaking the bond of his or her passions, as if they alone impeded us by controlling free expression. Secular solutions have urged us to try a completely unrestrained indulgence of passion. The premise is that unsatisfied desire itself blocks free expression. At the other extreme some religious disciplines seek to get rid of passion completely. We can compromise on this issue by admitting that there is such a thing as addiction and a bondage to passions. Nevertheless, our aim need not be elimination but rather the control of emotion. We need an understanding and a purging (vs. indulgence) of passion.

Our aim is to convert natural tendencies so that feelings do not war with one another and destroy but instead are harmonized in one direction of flow. We need to rid people of their emotional and mental delusions in order for free expression to take place. The issue is how to accomplish this, particularly since "reality" has no one agreed-upon description. We must form an acceptable picture of the nature of things before any vision of reality can free us, and we cannot do this if we keep insisting that there is one true theory, all the while many are possible.

We begin with a bundle of paradoxes and contradictions both in our minds and in our emotional lives. The question is: how far can the intellect go toward getting itself out of this? As Zen suggests, perhaps we need to go beyond intellection and passion to emptiness. Yet on the other hand, if reality itself is not contradictory, if all tension simply stems from the multiple levels of human life, then the intellect alone may not be sufficient to break these bonds. However, a purging of the emotions and a training of the will might be able to accomplish this.

Our release comes from no one source, neither by rising above nor by eliminating the intellect. Instead it stems from achieving a precarious balance of the three forces (intellect, will, emotion) in the self. If successful, these become no longer destructive and inhibiting but now are held in a balanced tension that makes forceful and creative expression possible. The self is the root of all evils, as the Zen Buddhist says. Nevertheless the self need not be eliminated. It can be cured so as to transform its destructive tendencies into a productive outflow, if we admit its multiplicity and aim for balance rather than reduction to a single level, whether this be intellect or emptiness.

We need to undergo a major operation in order to sever the knots within the intellect. We know that few people function at full capacity. A crippled intellect or emotional life is perhaps sadder and more difficult to deal with than the incapacitated body. Zen training aims to break our self-inflicted restrictions, and countless other remedies are offered to free the mind, some easy, some extremely rigorous and thus exclusive. For one thing, we all carry a heavy burden of the past. Much human suffering, and thus restricted power, stems from that weight. The major restraint on us is our inability to free ourselves from the past in order to give full attention to present and future. Freud proposed one method by which we could gain release from an inhibiting past; Christianity offers another. Buddhism in some of its forms is insistent on doing away with intellection, and it is true that thought is as often a road block to expression as it is a liberating means.

Unfortunately, the intellect is not by nature free, although not all have recognized this indiginous fault in the mind. The intellect gains its freedom only when it trains itself to the point where it can set itself aside so that actions flow freely without requiring thought. Fortunately the mind has the power to remove its own restrictive processes when the time comes to end self-dialogue. However, few people are able to control this power to suspend thought, since it requires the development of an increased force within the will.

The intellect seeks, so to speak, not its life but its death. However, "death" in this sense means a willful suspension of an otherwise endless production of thought and word when the time comes for decision, uninhibited action, and commitment. The Zen Buddhist vows not to rely on words but resolves to point directly at man's heart and at things, but this requires developing a skilled use of the intellect in order to achieve that moment of freedom from domination by endless thought. All forms of expression aim finally to set thought aside in order to move attention directly to its desired object.

Ironically, we must use words, thought, and speech for all instruction, even though our aim is to achieve an independence from them. We have no choice but to use conceptual means. Yet we know that some people will always remain trapped within the tools they are trying to use and never emerge to use their latent power of direct perception and expression. When the Buddha Nature is attained, we are told, we will be absolutely free from all bondage and thus will not be led astray because of linguistic complications, but this has been the goal of all philosophy from Plato to Wittgenstein.

Our major problem is that there is no one guaranteed route to follow but rather many. One avenue works for some and not for others. Therefore, our only choice is for each of us to seek his or her own release, since no single doctrine is guaranteed superior to all others. However, we are not forced to seek this all alone. We can test the offered ways and write new versions of each gospel if necessary. Only blind isolation and arrogant self-reliance are dangerous. We need not fear a free exploration of all those avenues opened to us by past instruction.

If a freedom from reliance on thought is the goal, and if a resulting powerful expression is the prize, silence obviously has its place, since thought and language are neither ultimate nor always self-validating instruments. Yet silence cannot be communicated unless we go out of it, so that silence is not the final state we desire either. We need to be cautious in our use of words, so that they are not allowed to receive a sanction of ultimacy. The aim of speech is to make us go beneath words to dig out that from which they arise and that toward which they move. In such a case, words can never be true in themselves, and personal experience is everything. Speech and writing may induce experience; in fact some of our most important ranges of experience would be impossible except for the stimulation provided by these forms of expression. The aim is not to confront people with either words or art forms but to induce understanding by a variety of means.

Zen's aim is to leave one's mind free and unobstructed, and so do we all wish for that state. The issue is whether one discipline is applicable to all, or whether the roads to freedom are many, even if the paths to confusion are more numerous. Language is the most treacherous instrument the mind ever invented. It can conceal and trap us in its maze, while at the same time it has the ability occasionally to raise us beyond our own natural powers of perception. But we have a choice. We do have other human instruments at our disposal, e.g., physical discipline and various human arts.

In the end language is unavoidable. It is that instrument which men must either master or else be overpowered by it and lost in its intricacies. Meister Eckhart feels that he can float high above space and time. He can be free above the multiplicity of things. At its root "mysticism" probably means just this freedom from natural restraints. Yet, language must be used in order to achieve this state of freedom.

Is it possible ever to break the restrictions of nature? That is perhaps our most important question. At least we know that some amazing people report the experience of such release. Mysticism is always bold in this way, and its practitioners use expressions that it would never occur to the average person to employ. For example, they claim direct insight into a God whose nature is vastly different from what we might ordinarily suspect, e.g., a "wasteland."

Evidently timidity and failure of nerve only guarantee our continued bondage to a limited range of expression. A strong will is necessary, although will is not in itself sufficient to guarantee liberation. Like reason, it can run amuck in its demands too, but no release is possible without an intense nurture of the will's power and then a focusing of its direction. Yet, the direction given to this effort is crucial if we are to achieve free expression. Too often the will's power is allowed to remain internal or self-directed. This simply leads to inner explosions, not to freedom.

It is, then, the self we need to be free from. We can agree with Buddhism. We will never have perfect liberty of mind until our attention can be directed outward and the self forgotten. Some assert that this must involve its destruction or loss, or at least a rising above the distinction between self and other. This might be a necessary means or stage, but the issue is not so much the absence of self as whether we can be released from the constant self-attention that restricts expression. Free expression requires an ability to go out from oneself. We need to learn to be concerned only with another person, object or event so that we can form our expressions free of self-involvement. Since immediate self-attachment is natural, as child development theories tell us, the conversion of the self is the maturing of the self, that is, its turning away from adolescent self-absorption.

The pedagogical question is whether we can ever teach without complete dependence on the sound of words. The basic point is even more subtle and more difficult than merely not using words by retreating either into action or silence. Words may be used, but how can they be employed sparingly, interspersed with space? We do not want attention diverted to the verbal structure itself, which is our tendency today, but we want our attention released to the immediate confrontation of the mind with its desired object. Words do form structures. These patterns and intricacies are amazing and even fascinating to study on their own. But the mind must not be disoriented so that it takes this artificial product as its ultimate object of study, or else it will lie trapped within itself. Words mirror the very structure of the mind that we wish to break down and set aside, but we cannot do this without beginning our study by using verbal structure itself—that is the irony of the human situation and our self-imposed labyrinth.

How can we bring ourselves through words to silence without being caught in the process so that we never emerge from the verbal circle? This could never be done if words themselves did not have that amazing property of bringing us into relation with silence. When this happens, knowledge is no longer an increasingly cumulative burden. Rather, it is now borne silently and lightly and used effectively. So much knowledge merely sits on the mind like a heavy weight. It decreases effective action rather than encouraging movement. It allows one to drift about in an intellectual fantasy world, one that is fascinating but unable to affect reality. Interestingly enough, free will is the crucial factor that can make the difference in effective outlet. Once it gains release, it is the operative will and not the understanding that marks man as being in the image of God. It is not

God's vast understanding that makes him divine. It is his control of will that enables him to act by cutting the cord of reflection.

Mysticism means many things, but its root meaning is "a purging of the intellect." This is also the sense in which mysticism is applicable to God, since he can accomplish this at will, and we seek such a purging too. Our minds must be cleared of prejudice and convention, but this cannot be done by a completely rational process as Descartes thought and hoped. All mystical disciplines aim at such cleansing, and people need this because God alone is self-cleansed. He achieves a constantly free mind unrestricted by information. We begin with the self first, but the trap into which many fall, including Descartes and Kant, is that our aim should be to induce self-forgetfulness. The self-emptying of which God is capable must be imitated by us, or else self-attention will restrict us and mislead the mind's attention all our days.

We speak of love in this connection, but we know that the insidious problem involved is that love instinctively emerges as self-desire and self-gratification. Love is capable of being transformed to an un-self-conscious outflow, but this happens only through suffering and an acquired discipline—one capped by the descent of a non-natural spirit (see Chap. VI-B). The seat of love is the will. Thus, it is more the will that needs reformation in order to provide the effective release for action than the understanding needs a probing of its depths (Freud) or an analysis of its structure (Kant). Love depends altogether on the will, and this tells us where we should turn our attention, if this is the point at which human nature needs reversing. If to have more will is to have more love, such increase can only become a release if the demonic tendencies of the will are first broken and turned away from self-protection and gratification.

The mind has a tendency to become engrossed in and thus tied down to its peculiar interests. Our goal should be to keep a free mind in all we do, but it is rare that a person can do this without passing through struggle and training. It does not matter whether our discipline is self-achieved or the result of following some established strict program. It requires great diligence if neither circumstance nor current involvement is to bother us; yet that is our goal.

If in God (or Being) there is action at the center, our soul's essense will involve action too, and the question is how to release this power. We know this can be done if we watch the creative few. Yet we also observe that the process is seldom tranquil or unaccompanied by an inner struggle for release. The jungle of thought and passion in which we live grows back at a furious pace once it is cleared; tangles are renewed as fast as they are cut away. We must constantly fight against this reversion tendency, if thought and passion are not to restrict the soul's view. Otherwise our soul is turned back upon itself, which is just where its attention should not be.

God acts without instrumentality, without ideas. However, it does not follow that this is because he has neither willing agents nor an infinite intellectual calculating machine that contains in its storage units every possible and impossible idea. But divinity knows that, when the time for decision arrives, all mediums must be set aside if thought is not to become self-embroiled. Rationality itself never yields us only one course of action as the result of its idea-calculation, however much rationalist philosophers hoped it would. Therefore, the freer you can become from ideas, the more sensitive you are to God's inward mode of action, and the more open you are to uncomplicated expressions of love and to actions that build and sustain rather than deteriorate and destroy. Of course, the irony involved here is that freedom requires that we first learn to obey, a paradoxical lesson that many refuse to accept. Lacking internalized discipline, they waste themselves in impulsive and noncumulative behavior. Only those who learn a rhythm other than their own can be free—but we still remain basically free in the initial choice of the pattern we elect.

What is the essence of God? Our answer: the struggle for freedom. If so, God will be missed or else seem lifeless if approached solely by a rational analysis of his (or our) thought content and speech. To say this is not to demean words, but to place them back where they belong, that is, as instruments. Some words are as important as deeds, but such expressions are rare and hard to discover. We treat certain words as deeds because they affect others that way, whether constructively or destructively. The doors of perception may or may not need to be enlarged, whether by drugs or ritual, but they certainly need to be cleansed so that everything can appear to us as it is. It is important for us to achieve such direct apprehension, and it is not easy to accomplish. So much human energy goes into cover-up activities and into learning the art of appearing as one is not. Fear cannot love, so that the cure of fear is more important for the mind's release than new ideas.

> Love seeketh not itself to please
> Nor for itself hath any care
> But for another gives its ease
> And builds a heaven in Hell's despair.
>   Blake: *Songs of Innocence*[1]

Blake's poetic insight is correct. He only needs to add that this selflessness is not love's natural direction, which is far from pure. If left unconverted, love tends to create hell and to make the ego sick with self-attention. Once reformed, love can become pure, but it is not born free. The gospel of allowing free expression for every impulse is exciting, but it also creates havoc in its wake. When desire simply spreads formlessly, it induces tensions too much for most to bear. Since the power of the will cannot be similarly extended, we eventually lose control and become the victims of desires that know no restraint.

The better we understand our own ignorance the greater our learning will be. That is, we discover that there is nothing the mind cannot reach and embrace. The human mind at its zenith can match God, and it wins in its struggles as often as it loses. But the "unavoidable ignorance" we finally encounter is both our impossibility to control simultaneously all that is available to us and our inability to free ourselves from that self-attachment that restricts action. Absolute truth is beyond our grasp; that is the central proposition of mysticism. This is not because any possible idea is in itself beyond our range, but because our power of control cannot match the depths of our mind. Freedom comes on occasion, like mystical union, to the few, but this is not sufficient to lift the restraint placed on the range of power of most. The release from the self-concentrated fight to protect our desires and satisfactions is available only to the few. The protective battle unleashes furious forces, but it also restricts our freedom to love.

Rollo May agrees that "in the failure of will lies the central pathology of our day, and that our time should be called the 'age of the disordered will.' "[2] Yes, we want and we seek the gift of freedom as perhaps no age has ever done, but this places tremendous burdens on the individual. The paralysis of the will is one ironic result of this strain. All around us people make violent thrusts for freedom that simply explode into destruction, because there is no accompanying will strong enough to sustain itself in the vacuum created when restraints are thrown off. Hate and self-satisfaction must be purged from the self first, or its natural response to new freedom will simply be an orgy of self-gratification followed by a vengeance that destroys its own ground. Human beings must be converted before they can handle freedom. They need and they seek free expression. However, the natural inner-concentrated and fettered self cannot handle such naked power without directing it inward. This movement simply converts the power of freedom into the force of destruction.

Freedom calls for a prior mortification and cleansing of the self, although this is not a mortification that denies life but one that creates liberation. The natural self-gratifying ego should be abandoned, and it must die before a self capable of governing freedom can be born. Without suffering it is not possible to attain freedom, but this must be a suffering aimed at self-release, not one that builds on hatred and hidden revenge.

There is, of course, no such thing as "slow freedom." All who achieve release report that it is like a sudden new birth. All birth takes place in a moment, and there is no halfway measure. We are slaves until we are fully free. As long as we hold on to ego gratification, full release is not possible. We must liberate ourselves from the impediment and fatigue of ideas and thoughts as well as from self-erected passions. We reach out until finally we care nothing about even desire or thinking or meditation. Descartes could not risk such release from thought.

Freedom of the soul is our goal, but what is the soul's essential being? It is neither a body nor a state nor an experience of body, as Spinoza thought. It is act and creation. If this is true, whenever thought or desire impede this action, they block the soul's transformation to its essential being. The soul is not naturally born that way (free) but needs to be converted. Solid souls are made not born. But their essence is given to us in the form of a goal. We are only deceived about this because so often, looking at the natural human state, we see only a bundle of moving, tangled feelings and thoughts. The project is to become a free self. Therein lies our sought-after essence as men and women.

B. New Life

Those who seek new life are not confined simply to church members or even to those who express a religious interest. Unfortunately, all who receive renewed life are not within formal religious communities. The intensity needed to propel a successful religious search often tends to be self-defeating. Religious intensity puts stress on the individual and on that person's needs, and this is the very opposite of the direction needed for the release to new life. Although individual confession and repentance are the necessary prerequisites of change, ironically once again a religiously morbid stress on either sin or virtue defeats the whole enterprise. The self can be reformed to new power only by pressure away from its existing center. Whatever induces concentration on the self, whether a mournful dwelling on past sins or a Freudian rational analysis of the past, may be necessary as a prelude. Yet, no new life is possible unless this direction can be broken and reversed.

If Siddharth, the Buddha's name, means "every wish fulfilled," humanity's only common wish may be to achieve a regenerated life. The world is filled with techniques that claim to achieve this. Some are moderately successful; some are superficial and fraudulent because they promise more than they can provide. The young are naturally less interested in techniques of this type, since at the moment they are more interested in self-realization than in fundamental change. A few who are still young already feel impulses moving irresistibly to defeat their wishes, and so they are religiously disposed to seek a future change even while still youthful. Yet, it is hard to accomplish this without having gone through suffering and some lost battles. Only purgation can prepare us to release the iron grip we hold upon ourselves or induce us to relax our self-protection sufficiently to allow basic change.

In any preparation for new life, we must ask about the role of asceticism, the ancient religious tendency to insist on denial and self-chastisement. Since the aim of such stringency is to cut off those desires of the self that center on its ego, at least some asceticism or denial of pleasure is needed as a first step. To seek to receive a new self and yet at the same time to hold on to all our original desires and conceits—that is the height of frustrating self-defeat. Yet what should the specific means of denial be, and do these in themselves automatically produce new life? These questions remain as the religious puzzles that deny universal solution and require individual resolution. The aim is to make the self into an illuminating light rather than an obscuring force, but the issue is whether this can be accomplished solely by relying on yourself.

Desire undoubtedly lies at the root of human suffering, but the question is whether our aim should be to remove it so that passion dies and human suffering is put to an end in this way. Or, should ascetic denial aim to alter the direction of desire so that passion is diverted away from the self and becomes compassion? We are hampered by ignorance as well as by desire. Yet sometimes to learn more is simply to increase suffering, so that one might say God's infinity of understanding commits him to more suffering than any human nature could bear. Thus, just as desire is not eliminated but is merely redirected, so also as ignorance is removed suffering increases. That is, this happens unless the power of the will to control is increased proportionately at the same time. If new knowledge means new life and heightened action, only in that way can suffering be increased but still contained.

Our aim is not to suffer less but to suffer less destructively.

There is an ego-personality that is naturally born and naturally increases in the power of its demands. However, the aim is to cut off this power by an ascetic denial that does not strangle but simply redirects the flow of power outward and away. The mind that discriminates is in fact our true mind, but it is the distinguishing and dividing and calculating aspect of mind aimed at self-pleasure and protection that often makes this mental capacity seem to be a fault. When the discriminating function is freed from its slavery to self-satisfaction, it is released to create new life. We can eliminate the "observing self," not because there really is none of substance, but because it can become un-self-reflective through outward action.

Due to its natural construction the self becomes a block. But it need not be eliminated. It simply needs to be returned to its pristine state and then rebuilt so that its attention is directed away from itself. It is the restrictions the ego has built up around it that need removing, not the self. It can be transformed to operate beyond these bounds. Peace comes to the self when the struggle between self and object subsides. Then the intense relationship that weds all objects to self-interest is dissolved, and our interest is allowed to focus on objects in themselves. Kant thinks this is impossible, but that is because he cannot relax his self-analysis and ignore the mind by studying directly what lies outside of it. The individual ego naturally asserts itself strongly, but our aim should be to turn this power around to overcome itself. We want to redirect its attention and to convert its power to peaceful means, rather than to allow it to continue on in an ego-induced warfare.

When the Buddha attained his supreme enlightenment, we are told, he was in his sitting posture. Since few can spend that much time in the lotus position, the issue is not whether this is effective for some but whether new life can be discovered in an active posture too. Meditation has one danger in that initially it increases self-reflection. Activity has the opposite pitfall of not allowing us time for self-evaluation. No posture, evidently, in itself either enlightens or provides new life. Thus, regeneration can come in the midst of noise as well as in silence, although perhaps the contrast provided by two poles, e.g., action-rest, noise-silence, is itself the main necessity. Only that one is lost who thinks that any one of these poles is all of life.

Self-rejuvenation never comes from mere listening and thinking. Prior cultivation of willpower is crucial to any redirection of the natural flow of attention. True knowledge may transcend all modes of expression. It is unable to confine itself to any one form, neither art nor ritual language. Yet, since all mediums must be employed, words are just as likely a vehicle as silence, and action can be as insightful as pure rest. The way of the Buddha may be to remain all the time in absolute emptiness and calmness. Yet, as many Buddhists say, that is self-defeating if taken as an exclusive end. A mind may be pure only when it is above purity and impurity, but it also may be renewed when the will balances thought and redirects desire outward. To have the mind thoroughly void of all conditions is one essential experience, but so is the action of the will that restructures our inner self-direction.

Even harboring the thought of purity breeds nonpurity, which means that new life does not depend on achieving any one state, e.g., rest, as Aristotle thought. Instead, new life consists in holding the self in suspension among all states and allowing it to settle on no one. This accomplishment requires first of all an infusion of power into the normally weak will, which so often is ready to settle for some one proposed ideal state. The philosophical prejudice is that thinking alone can solve our problem. However, as we ordinarily use the term, thinking is not the means we need. Our aim should be to achieve a new form of feeling, a disposition of the will, and this is harder by far to build and to control than thought. When new life is opened, will and emotion blend with thought.

Such a life can never be the simple product of intellectualization. This is why Freudian analysis, which relies entirely on verbal exchange, is good at exploration but is less successful at directing a fusion of emotions that can produce both new direction and the energy needed to move away from the ego-centered self and its past. The mind demands "yes and no" as answers to its questions. Unless we can break through such a neat antithesis, we can never hope to live a life of freedom. Our problem is not so much that the mind has delusions that must be fought out within the mind, as both Freud and Spinoza want to do. Any intellectualism risks self-defeat by first putting too much emphasis on the mind as the seat of the problem and then going on to place too much stress on the intellect as the sole means for its resolution. The intense effort of the mind, even for mind control, is not so much for what we need as a balance of thought, will, and emotion. This allows human power to form non-destructively.

If we could ever sever the bonds of desire, we might live in peace, but we would also live unproductively. In its own way, to seek to be rid of desire is as selfish as to seek a constant satisfaction of desire. Such emptying of the self is not likely to become a goal as long as we are successful in keeping abreast of the demands of our desires, and some can do this quite nicely. Desires do not so much need to be overcome as to be controlled by will and kept at a distance so that desires do not constantly circle around the self and absorb its energy. The "being" that we want to become is a salvation, since we seek that new state because of its power to produce change. The way of salvation is not so much increased knowledge, although that is involved, as it is a release of the emotions from their natural bondage. This is a mysticism, but it involves the transcendence of emotion more than reason.

Song, symbol, cult, and silence are all instruments of mystical change. In this case, mysticism simply means that which breaks and reverses our natural directional flow. A mysticism of the intellect is a teaching mysticism. It hopes to accomplish its ends by instruction, since it is the structure of the human mind that appears to need the greatest overcoming. To one who has seen a face of God, the aim is to do what he can to become pleasing in God's sight. This means the confession and repentance of all self-centeredness that has damaged others (i.e., sin), plus an ascetic attempt to reform desire by restricting its fuel. Fire is our symbol here, for through fire everything changes, so that we call on fire when we want everything changed. "Next time the fire", God threatens us. The crucial question, however, is whether the purging force of fire can be held in check short of its destructive tendency to consume everything in sight.

As is evident from the daily newspaper, neither a world nor a person going up in flames contributes much to the needed reconstruction. Eckhart wants us to put disinterest higher than love, but that depends on whether God's habitat lies in purity and unity as Eckhart thinks it does due to his disinterest. God basically may not have much in common with the disinterested mind, although he may use "empty nothingness" as a purging state which the self must pass through in order to loosen all its natural efforts at self-protection. Disinterest may act like a divine fire, and still it may not so much lie at the center of God's nature as it is his instrument of transformation. The aim is to liberate the deep-lying powers of the self and to unify them into one conscious life. The goal is a self neither merely intellectual nor volitional nor emotional, but to be balanced in an effective fusion that allows new expression.

George Fox, the founder of Quakerism, calls it "the opening." Unusual psychological phenomena may be involved, but to argue over their rational acceptability is surely to be distracted from the main question.

> The significant features of the experience are the consciousness of fresh springs of life, the release of new energies, the inner integration and unification of personality, the inauguration of a sense of mission, the flooding of the life with hope and gladness, and the conviction, amounting in the mind of the recipient to certainty, that God is found as an environing and vitalizing presence.[3]

Such an experience involves the whole self as it is now transformed, and this is hardly the simple result of an intellectual quest or the achievement of tight mind control.

Philosophy rightly by its nature pursues understanding. Yet religiously speaking, it is chastened in this constant quest by the realization that the effect upon the soul of many religious documents and rituals, e.g., the Kabbalah, is not at all dependent upon their being understood. If we grant to the Enlightenment the premise that some mysteries are destructive and enslaving and need rational scrutiny, it is still true that the reformation of the self is not entirely an intellectual project, nor is its success measured by the extent of rationalization we achieve. Once the Western religions are demythologized, the mysteries of the East seem personally more effective for those who seek new transformations—except perhaps to the East to which they are already too familiar.

Self-perfection, it seems, is achievable neither byself-concentration nor by transcending the structures of the self into nothingness. It is attainable only through other selves. Thus, the humility of our situation is that we are forced to become dependent when it comes to the matter of achieving the self we want. The road to God leads through humanity, and he is to be found there more than in either ritual or emptiness. Humankind is God's only link with his creation. Thus it is also the key to creation's mystery, but the crucial sin most people fall into is to try to study either nature or God only as it is reflected in themselves, e.g., Descartes. The trick is one of reversal. We need to study both ourselves and God and find renewal outside the self through our ability to attend and respond to needs other than our own. God can voluntarily empty himself of self-concern. We must learn to do so or else we will be forced to that door by self-inflicted suffering.

To be a spiritualist means to gaze mostly into the future. Even though deception is involved in this practice, we risk self-defeat if we do not see the danger involved in total concentration either on the present or on a reconstruction of the past. "Let the dead bury the dead" means let the self be free of its recriminations and constant reassessments. The need is to turn the self's attention to a future life and to discerning its shape, even if astrologists and mediums are not our best guides. We look back only in order to sense those times in which we have felt new life breaking forth, e.g., in the Apostolic Church. In this way of reflecting on the past we gain some notion of what new life means and how it might arrive again. The Holy Spirit, as a moving *force* is, however, always superior to the *record* of the work of the Holy Spirit. To cling exclusively to any religious record or to analyze it exhaustively is seriously to misdirect our attention once again, even if that record is a holy Bible.

Spirit is experienced as driving power. The question is how we prepare for such consciousness, not how it was once recorded. Any answer is "error ridden" as it comes to us from the past. If our problem is to become daily aware of the possible fresh revelation of God, we cannot avoid excesses and mistakes —that bane of all rationalists and traditionalists. Cultivating such awareness and even risking false possession by demons is surely the only avenue to new life. Otherwise, we are left to the ultimately depressing task of constantly going over old ground. As we explore backwards, we are constantly amazed that the record and its surviving rituals grow more and more lifeless and are less and less able to transform us once again. If God is free, to learn the record of his past actions by heart is only a part of knowing how he may act again.

If the word "martyr" is applied to anyone who lives a truly self-sacrificing life, martyrdom is the only route to new life, except that we should not treat "death" so visually and physically. What rules do each of us need to hold to personally if God is to be pleased? Unfortunately, the answer is that no uniform sacrifice is prescribed for all. "Let the sacrifice fit the crime." If psychiatrists find that the chief block to therapy is the patient's incapacity to feel, one ascetic sacrifice is to give up protecting feeling by refusing to extend it. Martyrdom is to feel too much, although this is not true if all feeling simply centers in the self. Destruction comes when one side, perhaps the demonic, usurps command and drives the person to disintegration. The power of the destructive should not make us withdraw into nonfeeling. It must be transformed into constructive action. That is, this must be our course if life rather than destruction is to come out of self-sacrifice.

When the self is explored, quiet darkness often appears at the depths, or so mystics report. The issue is whether this emersion in darkness is purifying, so that the self can love others more deeply and not simply itself as before. Of course, some hate their natural selves. That is, they either both love and hate themselves or else they are indifferent. Thus, the discovery of silence and darkness at the core of the self may cut the cords that either restrict emotion or allow it to be self-destructive. The perfect life and the true life both lie beyond the self's dark center in a fusion of will and emotion and thought into love's free outward expression. The life of happiness is a life of mixture. But as Plato pointed out, it is also a life that must be held in a delicate balance of proportions.

Plotinus is famous for his successful quest to convert the soul and thus to inaugurate new life. He tells us that our task is to work for liberation from this sphere.[4] There is another life available. It is an emancipated state whose quality is a progression toward a higher realm, toward the good and the divine. We can agree with Plotinus; we have ourselves seen the age of Man and Nature fail to provide us release within nature's bonds. But our question is: In what sense do we need liberation from "this sphere"? True, if we are to provide new life or liberation for great numbers, the destructive tendencies of the natural order will have to be broken and reformed in ways that open it more to human fulfillment. That may happen; some, e.g., Christians, believe it will.

For the present, our issue is whether any renewal of life is possible within this sphere as we now experience its powers and imperfections. Of course, we know that some human renewal is possible, because we see a few individuals break loose of restriction in order to exercise freedom and creativity. They turn suffering away from self-pity. They martyr their desires and bring fresh life into song or word or craft or action. Can we progress toward a divine realm by emancipation? Yes, but this raises the question of the divine life itself and what to share in God's own liberation would be like.

Does God always tend upward away from plurality and toward unity, as Plotinus thought? If he does not, the "liberation from this sphere," i.e., nature's inner self-orientation, may be possible without demanding passage to a "higher realm." God may be with us and very content to be here. He does not seek escape, as we sometimes do. This is because he has broken, or continues to break, his own self-absorption. Standing where he is, he may direct his attention freely to other persons and forms without self-attachment. His life is renewed because it is not self-centered, and thus it is not restricted in scope and vulnerable to constant loss.

Human beings match God's intellectual range, but they too

often restrict themselves in power and in will by being too inner and too self-reflective, that trap of all meditation. Whenever they break out of that self-directional bond, they can share more (but not all) of God's own power of self-renewal.

Notes To Chapter V

1. *The Complete Writings of William Blake*, "The Clod and the Pebble" (London: The Nonesuch Press, 1957), p. 27.

2. Rollo May, *Love and Will* (London: Collins, 1972), p. 16, quoting Leslie Farber.

3. Rufus M. Jones, *Spiritual Reformers in the 16th and 17th Centuries* (Boston: Beacon Press, 1959), p. 221.

4. Plotinus, *Eneads*, trans. MacKenna (Boston: Chas. T. Bramford), Vol. I, p. 167.

VI
Prayer

A. The Coming of the Kingdom

We began this essay by wanting love to be without pain. We found that, although love now cannot be without pain, it might still hope to move beyond pain one day. This requires us to convert ourselves to minister unto the needs of others, rather than always seeking to have others meet our needs. Mysticism must be involved in achieving such a transformation, because a change such as this requires a radical transcendence or reversal of the present ways of nature. This does not necessarily mean that God transcends rational grasp, but only that the change we seek demands that he control a power not now manifest to us. He wants us to change in place, not to remove ourselves from the world or its pressures. This involves moving beyond hope to a purified love, which requires a revolution in love's normally aggressive ways.

As we pursue this goal of transformation, it is necessary to follow some form of spiritual exercise. We cannot let every natural human satisfaction and impulsive action remain as it is and still expect change of a radical nature. A self-emptying, that passage through a "dark night" which purges the mind and the emotions of former content—this is a necessity. But all this cannot be done without submitting to a guiding discipline. There are many such "rules," but what we need to find is a "new rule" suitable for our own day. The new goal we have established is to become an instrument of peace. If this is how God's nature is now revealed to us, rather than as the warring God which we might suspect from watching how the natural world operates, our question is how humans can become such a God? Or is it really God who becomes human in any such transformation?

The experience we need is that of "conversion." This involves an opening to free expression and the experience of new life appearing within us. Such a quest ends in and involves prayer, since Christians are taught to pray for "the coming of the kingdom." This transformation and purification of love in human nature is what the coming of the kingdom represents. What, then, does it mean to pray for such an event, and how can such prayer open the way or speed the day of its happening? Sometimes this human goal has been thought to be happiness, and many religions have become successful because they promise happiness easily to their followers. Christianity is too cautious to offer pure happiness to its adherents in a hedonistic sense of pleasure. Yet one form of happiness is both the goal of prayer and the evidence of new life.

In some religions, the achievement of happiness is connected to the idea of loss of self and release from the world's dualities and tensions. Christians, on the other hand, are advised to love others, even their enemies. They are also cautiously told that this requires a prior self-love, although this can only be the love of a self now purged. We are to love others, not as we grasp them selfishly in order to hold on to our pleasures and satisfactions, but only as we have ourselves prayed to be transformed so that our love flows freely outward without hate or jealousy. To learn to love ourselves in this way is difficult because it is so unnatural. But this is what we pray for, and it is also the self-love that is necessary before we can love others in a like manner.

One who hates and despises oneself cannot love others except perhaps greedily, that is, in wanting to be like them. This does not mean that we must try to cover over our faults and our spiritually crippled aspects. It does mean that we need to free ourselves, or else be freed, from any prolonged morbid absorption involving the damage we have done. We must learn to accept love as a sign of forgiveness and then turn our attention away from a stifling self-concern over human error, "free at last." However, the Christian promise of life in such a new kingdom is qualified by saying that it cannot be fully realized now. In this postponement Christianity differs from some religions in which it is possible to achieve the desired states, e.g., enlightenment fully now, even if this state can only be acquired with great difficulty.

The key issue for Christianity is the assertion of God's instrumentality. We can and should enact some limited-to-extensive reforms now on both our selves and the relationships we sustain. Individually, persons whose actions and dispositions are converted to this new life are themselves the evidence of the possible future full state. God at present is only partially active (see Chap VI, section B), but he must become fully active at some future time. He must do this if nature's tendency to break some people to servitude and to restrict others is to be lifted and the whole of nature set free. Obviously those who do not have a God of sufficient power to work these reversals of nature's ways cannot be expected to believe in any such future state. Their confidence is only in what can be achieved now by a variety of human efforts.

Humanists, of course, rightly deplore any abject surrender of human effort simply in order to wait for some future divine intervention. This passivity is not what Christians pray for, nor is it what the Kingdom's present appearance means. Much new power is available now to those who will open themselves to receive it, and no human constructive effort is prohibited or blocked as such. The only question is: do we possess power sufficient to achieve and to sustain our announced goals? The whole course of nature cannot be broken and tamed by individual effort. If its routine is only diverted for a time, the issue remains whether such a drastic reconstitution is what is required before the forces of corruption can be brought under control and anything offered us other than limited human release. Some fortunate few achieve this now, but can humankind as a whole be set free except by the same fantastic power that shaped nature at its beginning?

Personal happiness, then, cannot be our single religious goal. The unrelieved suffering of humanity around us does not allow such callous behavior. Until humankind as a whole is free, we can be blissfully happy only by shutting ourselves off from the moral decay around us. Yet, the goal of emptying ourselves of self-concern and developing an outer direction of love requires us to maintain our sensitivity to those around us. This postpones full happiness until such time as all human agonies cease. Such present happiness as is possible comes from our sense of release and new life. It is our interim duty to spread human revival as widely as we can, and our trust is in a future day so transformed as to allow all nature joy.

The Buddha went about his country for forty-five years preaching and persuading men to follow his way of life. Jesus had a shorter time, but prayer in any case means the spread of the call to such a new way of life. In both instances, to call upon the name (Jesus Christ, or the Buddha of Infinite Light) is thought to be part of receiving the power of change. Prayer really takes the form of "calling on a name," that is, opening ourselves to the receipt of power. Sometimes it is said that our aim in prayer is to place the mind in control so that lesser desires will disappear. Tight control of the mind may produce enlightenment and as such this may be desirable. However, the control of will and passion and the conversion of love require greater power than mind alone can produce.

If Buddhism's fundamental idea is to pass beyond the world of opposites, that of Christianity might be said to be to break the power that directs the self inward and to create a new form of love. Christian love is one beyond pain because it flows outward without inhibition. The intellect is not the ultimate block preventing us from seeing God as he is. Mind does not so much need to be set aside or transcended, which some mystics claim, as it needs to be broken of absolute dominance. Then it can be balanced with love and held within a coalition that allows us at least limited freedom from self-restriction. Zen enlightenment does not come by ardent desire but often is the result of a trivial incident. In the West, Kierkegaard has called attention to the importance of the "accidental," and Christianity has asserted God's tendency to act unpredictably.

Both Stoics and Buddhists advise us not to let our peace depend on the hearts of human beings. But if outer-directed love is our aim, such a conversion, if it comes, ironically involves us in even greater sensitivity to needs other than our own. Of course, this does not have to involve letting our own new life depend on some form of approval from others. Such dependence on constant human evaluation and the need for support is eliminated when love is directed away from self-need. Our inner peace is no longer dependent on human love being returned to us in exact proportions to our outlay. Release is achieved by abandoning self-interest, but we do this by becoming increasingly sensitive to other human needs. At this point our peace is dependent on the degree of our confidence in some people now, and in God finally, to meet these needs. Martin Buber tells us:

> When senseless hatred reigns on earth, and men hide their faces from one another, then heaven is forced to hide its face. But when love comes to rule the earth, and men reveal their faces to one another, then the splendor of God will be revealed.
>
> in *Ten Rungs: Hasidic Sayings*[1]

Thus, if God's death has been announced in our time, it is people who are responsible, since God will reveal himself only when human love becomes selfless, and he will disappear when it is not. Yet Kazantzakis tells us that "the essence of our God is struggle,"[2] and this too is true. Both the human and the divine struggle aims at one thing: to relieve love from pain. To allow us to be free of self-interest and to create new life in the face of destruction—these are actions only a reformed love is able to accomplish.

Yet where prayer is concerned, we may have to pray all our lives without hearing much of an answer. God is guarded and sparing with his speech. He is capable of longer periods of silence than we can achieve even by long-practiced meditation. The real answer to any "proper" prayer, i.e., an unselfish one, is the opening out of love and the appearance of new life. Thus, we have to look more than we listen, if we are to see where such power may become manifest either around us or in us. Those who listen only to verbal communication may miss God's primary mode of response, i.e., a silent action to release our bonds. If so, the paths of approach to God can lie in desert isolation, in the cloister of the cathedral or in Zen meditation that achieves emptiness. But today the most logical place to approach God might be in the midst of daily life, since it is here that the power of change is to be observed more than in a scrutiny of interior states.

96 LOVE BEYOND PAIN

We must begin our change by entering a mood of inner absorption, but we must also hope for freedom from it and a reversal of this direction. Yet God never fully arrives, and perhaps that is why his presence is missed and prayer so often seems fruitless or unanswered. It is not his aim to fulfill our expectations but to turn our attention away from and cut off our attachments. To say this need not mean to join the chorus of the religiously disgruntled who complain about the vanities of the world's pleasures. To the ones who possess them, human-created pleasures can be luxuriously satisfying if sufficiently controlled. Thus, God does not soothe our hurt feelings as we expect and hope. Instead he moves to direct our attention away. If our minds remain rigidly fixed on our own list of injustices, we may miss God because he simply refuses to appear in such a setting.

If mystical meditative practice aimed only at individual satisfaction, it would be vain indeed and perhaps self-defeating. If, however, the goal is to affect others due to the individual transformation effected by such discipline, this may be God's only means of appearance or activity until the day he decides to remodel the world. It is true that, if the reversal of love is his aim, this can only be induced by the example of one so changed, beginning with a Buddha or a Christ. To this extent the self retains a modicum of selfishness too. That is, it is only through an altered self that love can find its needed expression and become an effective instrument. The issue is that the change cannot be prayed for within the self for the sake of the self but only for the power of its instrumentality. This is self-surrender but not self-loss.

Many have optimistically thought that once God is found the soul can have rest. Undoubtedly this hope is behind most original religious impulse. Of course, this depends a great deal on what God is like and what a meeting with him would produce. The search for rest is, of course, essentially a selfish desire. One ought to ask whether his God is the kind who grants such selfish requests or whether, knowing no rest himself, he is reluctant to grant it to others. Instead, he may when contacted move to turn people away from a concern for their own relief. He leads a movement away from rest and urges us to join the struggle for the reversal of love that turns it into an instrument of peace. We all know that to strive for peace introduces us to neither rest nor uniform praise. Devils bent on destruction hate peacemakers.

If we are allowed to be at rest in some desert or temple, our own sins may become clear and unavoidable, which is both why so many shun solitude as the worst evil and the Desert Fathers sought it. On the other hand, when we live actively among others we often do not see our own faults due to the distracting turmoil all around us. The question here is whether the religious aim should be to concentrate upon realizing the harm one has caused. True, if reversal and new life are the goal, this cannot come about without the preparation of repentance and the creation of a desire for change. Thus, a quiet facing of wrong, if not in the public press at least in prayer, is the *sine qua non* of any lasting religious disposition or hope of aid. However, the crucial moment comes after the confession is made. The question is, is our attention moved outward by this act, or is it only allowed to tie the self more tightly to its grievances with itself and with the world?

Jesus' attitude in the New Testament is rather clear. John the Baptist cries loudly for repentance. At times Jesus echoes this call as a necessary first religious step, but his direction and his emphasis seem to be more on accepting forgiveness. The resulting change is due to his realization that the actual concern of God's love centers on human affection. Jesus treads lightly over sin, whereas we either ignore it or wallow in it and so are unable to move beyond self-preoccupation. Thus, sin and harm are not the divine message. Human beings are enough aware of that. And even when we go to extreme lengths to deny wrong, this is less because we do not perceive it silently than that religiously we are not yet aware of a way to undo its damage.

If God encompasses all things, this includes contradictories, and also all of the natural order with its evil and its good. Our intellect can reconcile many but not all contradictories, since they never disappear from human life, even when the logician can develop techniques to eliminate them theoretically. More importantly, all is not so much resolved as dealt with. People develop an ability to deal with some contradictions, but they do not acquire God's power simultaneously to embrace absolutely all. One further trouble is that we tend to live in words, and it is relatively easy to devise mathematical and verbal systems that hold off contradictions. However, if God's nature is only partly intellectual and his expression is only at times verbal or mathematical, it is the resolution of contradiction *in action* that remains the greatest problem. We would rather live in words and formulae where the intellect can work wonders, but God demands resolution in act.

Even to appeal to our own experience is not enough. To find the knot broken in our contradictory behavior and to know release, this is amazing, but it is only a first stage. To receive and then to go out with a message, that is the next phase. The "word received from the Lord" is the resolution of love's contradictory ways, loving-hating, desiring-giving. But apostleship vs. receivership means to carry the key to love's release out to others as an offer of divine origin. Such a new person is only an instrument in whom any change is simply a first fruit and testimony of what is possible for all. Those, then, who sit in church pews pleading in prayer cannot begin to realize what is involved when they pray for "the coming of the kingdom." It means to offer yourself as an instrument. You pray to be one in whom love's bondage to itself has been broken, so that affection is now offered freely for another's support.

Gandhi put it simply. ". . . I shall never know God if I do not wrestle with and against evil even at the cost of life itself."[3] Quite simply, this is what prayer means. It does not mean verbal repetition or even interior struggle. True, the battle against evil always begins with its internal perception and recognition. However, the war is lost and prayer is stifled if the battle against evil remains an interior and a solitary skirmish. If it does, the self is concentrated on too much, even when the shift comes that turns the mind from the self or empties it of content. That is too intellectual and spiritual a battle. Insidiously it still leaves the self at the center of attention, even when it is in the focus of attention only by its claim to want to be set aside. Evil is real and exists outside the self in more than thought.

Only a purely intellectual God is found in any search for

him that moves solely along an interior way. That kind of God-of-the-intellect may provide some mental satisfactions for restless intellectuals. Thought may even reconcile the individual to one's own wrongdoing or quest for satisfaction. Even if such individuals find inner peace, our emotions create webs in which we strangle all the while physical violence and naked power brutalize and cripple those around us. A God who can resist this or convert such passion is not found in either thought or contemplation, however important both may be as disciplinary steps.

Effective prayer seeks to change itself into a mode of action against the evils that entrap others. The danger in pressing for action is Peter's, that it will draw a sword to resist force or seek power ostensibly to wield power for good. That can be done, of course. Power does corrupt even popes and presidents, and God is never seen in full face in either the ecclesiastical or the political battle. If evil is that which destroys life and inhibits or weakens human beings, then it renders them impotent to use the latent power they possess constructively. Admitting this, one does not need to go far to find an individual field on which to do battle.

However, our battlefront is more often a quiet and an individual struggle rather than one requiring election to any office. To recognize this fact is to learn what a life of true prayer is like. It means to pray for the conversion of love and the power to become an instrument of peace. We petition for release from the forces of self-absorption, and ask for the coming of the kingdom into a life torn with evil. Destruction often stems from a craving either to be loved or to possess power. Into this scene steps the prayer that love may be given freely instead of sought, and this is the only love that can move us beyond pain.

B. *The Descent of the Dove*

We are told that on December the 8th, when he was thirty-five years of age, the Prince became Buddha. Yet for most of us, it is difficult to date the descent of a new spirit so precisely. We wish this could be done, and religiously we are often disappointed because the anticipated change is less pronounced when it arrives. It is not quite what we expected, and it has less definite demarkations than we hoped. Zen enlightenment is achieved in an instant, and we know that many conversions are often decisive in a moment. Yet in calculating the descent of the dove, we need to ask whether change is always this datable. Is it also possible for the arrival of a new spirit to be slow and imperceptible at any given stage?

Of course, if both delusion and enlightenment originate within the mind, we know it is relatively easy to change a mental attitude decisively in an instant. Yet if body, emotion, and will require redirection as well as thought, it will be harder to transfer mental decisiveness into those spheres simultaneously. Any change that covers all aspects of the self often involves a slow and shifting struggle. We cannot clutch for our goal of change as if it were a thing, or else this desire itself becomes an obsessive obstruction. If in nirvana the mind is said to be at peace like the great ocean, the trouble is that the body and its passions and the will and its strengths do not so easily lend themselves to such restful repose as does the mind when taken alone. In this sense, the mind is deceptive. Its ease in adopting new attitudes misleads us into thinking that the other powers in the world and in our bodies will obediently follow the mind's lead. Most unfortunately this is seldom true.

Buddhism, of course, does not recognize a supernatural agency in the matter of change. Thus, less emphasis is put on the descent of new power than on the practical and systematic, spiritual and physical training of the individual. Buddhism can appeal to those without any confidence in a God or in his power to accomplish human reform. And the issue at stake here is important. Are we left to ourselves and the effectiveness of our own devised methods? Or, is all prayer and discipline simply a preparation? Is it an attempt to increase sensitivity and receptiveness for the arrival of a spirit that essentially descends outside our control and independently of manipulation by any human agency? If effort and persistence can accomplish our spiritual goal, all is different than it is if its arrival has the aspect of a gift received in no exact proportion to effort or desert.

It is one thing if we place absolute faith in our own inner

being, and it is quite another if authority does not come from within but is said to arrive unexpectedly from without. However, Christianity and Buddhism—and most religions—join in refusing to make the reasoning faculty of man final or absolute. This fact places all such religions in opposition to the philosophical rationalists. Religious conviction feels that reasoning may hinder the mind from coming into direct communication with itself, whether this is phrased as a block to enlightenment or as hostility to the arrival of a new spirit. The first lesson of all, then, is neither the abandonment of reason nor the downgrading of its obvious powers. We simply need to learn a caution about reason's effectiveness if we trust it as the sole instrument of religious enlightenment.

Inward composure is important, as is the exercise of the will and an actualization of its power. Reason probably cannot achieve this goal on its own, because its very nature makes it unable to surrender any power or control that it is not forced to. Thus, it is highly unlikely that one can think one's way to prostration at the foot of the altar. The crash, the joy, the unification of the personality—whether this comes from inner effort or as a gift from outside—is never solely a product of thought. However, it cannot be achieved blindly; reason must become reflective about its own limitations as well as its powers. Sometimes the condition for insight has been said to be that one must surrender all love of creatures in order to be changed oneself. Such a doctrine is too extreme. It is not the love of creatures that is to blame for our failures but only the question of whether we love them selfishly.

The forsaking of self, the resigning of self, is the crucial issue. Thus, love can and should be focused on creatures, since that is where God's affections are held too. To a certain degree, inward peace comes from such a resignation of self-ambition. This is peace, in the sense of setting down the heavy burden of self-defense and self-satisfaction, but the air is disturbed again if we are next directed to meet the human need we see around us. Disquiet now comes not from the self's unrelenting demands but from the delicate question of how and even whether one can move to meet such need. Even love's outward flow is not smooth, because it must first find an adequate vehicle for its expression. It also needs to find a way through the natural resistance of others in a manner that does not crush them. It is not easy to find an acceptance even for selfless love. The assistance we offer threatens the independence of any self who is still attached to his or her own pride and independence.

Ordinary passions are difficult enough, but if even selfless love were easier, life would be simpler. It is evident that Jesus met strong resistance to his own compassion, and one of our hardest lessons is to know how love can be made to help when we want it to. The same powers of defense that keep love selfishly directed spring to defend themselves against the acceptance of affection, since that too requires the lowering of the self's defenses and makes one vulnerable. Even our language becomes empty because God no longer speaks. To convey love in sign or symbol, let alone in act, is no simple matter.

If God speaks but little, so also are the expressions of love few in which its effect is rendered powerful. Too often love is weak and appears as itself feeble and in need. The difficulty is to find a suitable expression which neither distorts its intent nor demeans others. When God loves, then love is seen as powerful. And when God speaks, words become swords. Yet amazingly, these emotions and powers restore rather than destroy. That is the effect of, and the sign for, divine presence.

We know what the experience of love's conversion is like. Inwardly we are freed from hatred and ill will. A cleansing comes over us that we seemed unable to accomplish by our own trying. The result is a great lightness within, and a weight is lifted from the soul. This experience is like that which precedes death. At that time every exit is blocked and surrender becomes our only option. Except in this case the resulting feeling is not loss of life but life finally released to its own power. Love knows a thousand restrictions and inhibitions. That is, it is bound by these until the hatred which entangles it with jealousy is surgically removed. God's children journey inviolable, garbed in light—even to Dachau, or perhaps especially there.

When we consider the function of reason, we must consider the theme of the Cloud of Unknowing—love may reach up to

God himself even in this life, but knowledge is not able to carry us that far. Thus, to try to argue our way to God is curiously self-defeating. The problem is not even that simple. If love unleashed led straight to God, every debauchery would be a divine path, as some have hoped. Then the pressure on us to reason would not be so intense.

Love, as it is first given to us, is no better a path to God than to the devil. Love perhaps is even more naturally attracted to the latter, as any avid party-lover knows. Thus, our question is how to purify, alter or change love so that it can become a divine vehicle and the avenue for a more powerful disclosure of God than reason. Plato notwithstanding, Pure Beauty is not the guide we need, since that simply excites our erotic pleasures to their highest degree and ignites our desires to possess.

The experience of God we seek cannot be achieved simply by intellectual effort. In fact, few important human experiences can be, all of which works to the well-known impoverishment of the intellectually gifted. Yet the intellect's power of discernment and its classical ability to make and to hold distinctions, these all figure centrally in promoting a transforming experience. Those who advocate an intellectual way of training and approach to God have not been far from the truth. But to miss God slightly is as painful and as frustrating as to miss him entirely, just as a near victory is more disquieting than wholesale defeat.

Only intellect is able to distinguish love's damaging tendencies from its healthy drives and then hold both clearly apart to be discerned. The mind, therefore, can work subtly to cut love loose from its mooring to self-attachment. Love itself is too involved to see this separation as a necessity. Lamentably, the intellect can also inhibit us from releasing ourselves to enjoyment. If we lack control over the mind, we simply relax to enjoy life physically without thought. Intellect in league with the will can discern love's faults and move toward their correction.

Yet it is true that God is not apprehensible by the unaided intellect in spite of its crucial and indispensable functions, the recognition of which cultivates its conceit. We can never feel or see God completely clearly and distinctly. Descartes was right in seeing clarity and distinctness as properties belonging exclusively to the intellectual function. The cloud of darkness that is reported to surround God is not there because he cannot be known. It remains there simply because the intellect that disperses darkness is neither the sole nor the adequate means of divine approach. This fact quite naturally leads us to conclude that God's nature is not wholly mind, or else the intellect would have exclusive rights to control all access to him. What is centrally love must be known by love and by a love as free from self-protection as its object. What is will must be felt as the presence of a power more decisive than our own.

Yet love as it appears on the streets when darkness comes is not a sufficient means of access to God. How then can love be remodeled to become an appropriate instrument to aid the intellect in its ancient search for completion? To love God truly one must first love people, and this can rarely be accomplished by the religious tendency to turn away from human involvement. Of course, we withdraw religiously to solitude because we sense the destructive selfishness latent in our love of others. Thus, our goal should be to hold on to that love and to that direct human contact, all the while we seek to cut the cord of self-attachment and thus free love from self-entanglement. Once this is accomplished, such love becomes a way to know God by loving him in an unencumbered way.

Our aim is to experience the descent of the dove, but our problem in appraising charismatic gifts is the ancient one: how can one distinguish demonic possession from divine ecstatic powers? The two are not always together, but still they are frighteningly close at times. In fact, they are so intertwined as to make many reject all spiritual heightening of emotion in order to be safe from its latent deception. Saint Paul offers a simple rule here, and it fits our quest for love beyond pain. He discounts any "gifts of the spirit" and experiences that do not help other souls, c.f., his letters to the Corinthians. Consider just how often the claim to religious gifts is entirely selfish or is centered on meeting only the individual's own demands. Then we realize how rare the descent of the Holy Spirit is, but also how simple it is to distinguish its presence by using this rule.

Contemplation is the term the Latin Church used for what we call mysticism, but this only raises for us the question of the role of contemplation in our various approaches to God. Does meditation spring from a selfish desire of the individual to achieve personal release? In a Christian understanding of both love's ways and the reform of love we need an avenue to God. Such a self-centered beginning is doomed to defeat unless a reversal of affection occurs, although ecstatic union is not excluded. Renunciation has always been the key to the contemplative way. If this renunciation goes so far as to strike at the self-interest and the comfort of the contemplative, the Christian God has a chance to appear again whenever merely personal desire is renounced.

Ascetic regularity and monastic discipline spring from the contemplative's passion for the direct association of the soul with God. When we step back in some horror over the egoism we discover to be involved in this goal and realize the selfishness implicit in this passion for divine union, we come to question both the goal and the means. Then we must revise our views on the role of ascetic practice and discipline. If extensive surgery must be performed on love in order to make it into a suitable divine instrument, ascetic denial and discipline become necessary if we are to endure such a painful enterprise. However, if the forced union of the soul with God is rejected as itself an inherently selfish desire, ascetic denial becomes a practical matter of determining where the individual has need for control, e.g., in alcohol, sex, drugs, desire for prestige. In this case discipline does not so much itself transform love as simply prepare us to receive a new spirit.

George Fox always thought of the Lord's spirit as accompanying him, and his *Journals* report that the Word of the Lord was like a fire in him.[4] It should be so if, as Quakers believe, every .man is enlightened by the divine Light of Christ. Quakerism is a religion of first-hand experience. It is based not primarily on historical happenings but on inward events, and this is true in all cases that depend on the transformation of love by the arrival of a new spirit. Patience and perserverance hold the key to contemplative fulfillment. This openness to receive spiritual gifts, which must first be scrutinized for its selflessness, is the mark of the one who accepts the necessity to transform love before the divine quest can succeed. To think that Jesus can be found today by a "historical quest" involves some very dubious assumptions.

Of course, if we define contemplation as "nothing else than a secret and peaceful and loving inflow of God,"[5] we can see a possible rapproachment between the reform of love and the desire for divine union. What may and often does begin as a selfish individual quest for satisfaction can be turned around. This happens when God's stubbornness is encountered, when his love refuses to allow itself to be forced no matter how rigorous the life-style or how persistent the demands. The purging of the self leads to the purging of the desire, whether it is the desire for union or the desire to receive God's love. If one's own tensions are relaxed in this way, the fulfillment of contemplation can come as well on the ghetto streets as in the cloister or the jail cell. It depends on beginning the reverse flow of love's crude direction and not on our place or posture.

Such an alteration can take place among human beings, once the necessary change in desire is realized. The love that leads us to God comes not from the soul's intense quest to see him—which is an essentially selfish wish—but from the kind of love that can only be exhibited to another human being. Thus, to love God alone or in solitude is not possible. Kierkegaard tried it and nearly drove himself mad. Of course, the lessons learned in solitude should be those of how love can be reformed and how it now must be humanly expressed. Once this is realized, God may appear in the form of anyone whose needs are ministered to selflessly. Nevertheless, his presence may just as easily be missed, since our attention has now shifted away from intense striving for transcendantal vision and simply settled on human pain.

Thus, when God does not appear to us on request as our primitive and grandiose religious sentiments first demand, it is easy to miss detecting his presence. Probably the dove that descended on Jesus' shoulder at the time of his baptism was discerned by few. At least only one evangelist reported it. The presence of God's spirit with Jesus in his ministry was discerned by some, but surely it was simultaneously overlooked by many, including those who crucified him. True, Jesus achieved considerable popular acclaim for a time, but this was the perennial selfish side of religion manifesting itself. His recognition came as the crowds' needs and desires were ministered to, and it evaporated as soon as the denial of their own hopes and aspirations was demanded. Crucifixion of the self is a normal early religious goal only for those who are possessed of an excessive morbidity. We start first with happier religious expectations.

Jesus did not reject the human desires his followers pressed upon him, and neither did he refuse himself all satisfaction. His ascetic rigors were surprisingly few, and his contemplative discipline was not obvious, or at least it required only slight detachment from crowds. When the holy spirit comes, however, it is purging in its effect and self-releasing when divine and not demonic. One can be possessed by evil as well as by holy spirits, but the release from self-concern seems to be the simplest way of cleansing demons, since it leaves them no food to feed upon. And the resulting painless love is the surest sign of divine presence.

God is hard to discern, not because he so transcends rational structure, but because he is so selfless in his love, even though he has the power to be supremely selfish in his demands. He is surprisingly careless about where and with whom he allows himself to be seen or how his emotions are made evident.

Notes to Chapter VI

1. *Ten Rungs: Hasidic Sayings,* trans. Olga Marx (New York: Shocken Books, 1962).

2. Kazantzakis, *The Saviors of God*, trans. Kimon Friar (New York: Simon & Schuster, 1960), p. 92.

3. In *The Essential Gandhi*, ed. Louis Fischer (New York: Vintage Books, 1962), p. 208.

4. George Fox, *Journals*, ed. Rufus M. Jones (New York: Capricorn Books, 1963).

5. Saint John of the Cross, *Collected Works*, trans. Kavanaugh and Rodriguez (London: Thomas Nelson and Son, 1964), p. 318.

VII

Steps to New Life

A. Prologue

We want to outline the steps we must take to reform love, since this project is the key to opening up new life. However, we run up against the problem of God and the mind's relationship to him, since God must play a key role in any eventual human transformation. If we are wrong about God, or if the mind is blocked or blocks itself in its approach, all our hope for substantive change fails. In an age in which God has been all too seldom heard and felt, we need to ask if this absence is not itself the primary reason so few of late have turned away from destruction. Perhaps our mind today both blocks us in our relationship to God and in like manner inhibits any decisive personal reform.

If all this is true, we need to understand why it is so. To recognize the intellect as being partially at fault is not to turn violently anti-intellectual. We must still use the mind to understand both its self-frustration and its possible mode of reform. Fortunately, the mind can understand things other than itself. That is, it can if it does not allow itself to be caught in its own self-reflective nature. It must explore more than its own structure if it would be effective in the world. The forces operative outside us are more than simply mental.

Is it possible, we ask, that the mind by its own nature may never be able to understand God fully? This might be true for several reasons. First, arguments have a way of going round and round and of being less than conclusive, particularly where God is concerned. Sometimes this has been thought to be because God transcends rational bounds; perhaps his nature involves some union of opposites that lies beyond the distinctions used by mind. This may be so, but another explanation might be this:

By concentrating on arguments the mind always misses the fact that God's nature is dominated by emotion and will.

If reason is simply a part of God's nature and the instrument he uses to form his expressions, then to follow only that route always misses discovering what God is really like. We will also remain dissatisfied with the results of our arguments just because we have an uneasy feeling that God must be more than this, if he is really to explain the depths and crosscurrents of the world we live in. The intellect touches only one side of life, and thus it naturally leaves us with an air of unreality where God is concerned.

Furthermore, it is not just the emotional side of the divine that reason may miss. Our lives are full of the high pleasures and the low destructions caused by the overflow of emotion. Thus, to add emotion to reason is not necessarily to guarantee that the result will be divine vs. evil. It is, then, the power of will we most often overlook. It is this which is most necessary for us to catch hold of if we would understand why emotion is nondestructive in God and how he is able to achieve a love beyond pain. In itself emotion tends as much to destruction as to construction.

In like manner, we trust in vain if we seek to find the source of our ethical norms in the intellect. Argument and mental energy, we all know, may be turned as easily into a plot to destroy as to some plan to promote human good. Reason in itself has no singular attraction to the good alone. Lamentably, it is a poor reforming force, as all of us know who have tried to argue either ourselves or another into a fundamental change. Reason does not have sufficient power to operate alone. By relying solely on argument we miss the reforming force in God that we all seek to emulate. That is, we must locate such a force if we are not simply to worship an idol made in the image of our own intellectual desires.

Some proponents of Zen have taken human reason to be impotent, but they do so for different metaphysical reasons. If good and evil are proportionally balanced, if being and nothingness are equal in power, then the mind's rational and discriminating tendency must be broken if any release is to be

gained. This might be a true picture if the emotions when directed to good and evil or to construction and destruction are also
equally balanced. But the fascinating fact is that people prefer
good and light and health and honesty at least just a little more
than evil and darkness and sickness and deceit.

Of course, just because we are held in bondage, the positive
balance of human attraction to good is often lost or thwarted.
We grow discouraged when we see that reason itself does little
more to support our good intentions than our impulse to destroy what opposes us. Human will is the key to this dilemma,
just as divine will is in God. Nothing can be done for reform
until the will yields. Our volitional side must indicate a serious
desire for reform and then support repentance and public confession. The will must end by throwing its power to the support
of our constructive emotions. If it does this, these sentiments
can gain dominance over evil, and then the mind can move reason
to the support of good ends.

God constantly reforms his love, just as human beings
should do. Only will can move reason and emotion away from
that self-preoccupation that binds emotion to our desire for self-
satisfaction. It is this tendency that makes the self unable to
love freely, and it also binds the intellect to argue for its own
peculiar goals without allowing it the power to free itself. Thus,
it is neither the reform of thought, as Descartes proposed, nor
its destruction nor its overcoming as Zen teaches, that is most
important. It is the conversion of the will. Once this power is
thrown into the project to transform love and free it from self-
concern, the intellect can be set free as it never will be by self-
analysis. This lesson we learn by observing Kant's brilliant but
internally bound critique of pure reason.

Thought and emotion are prisoners of the will and cannot
move beyond their status as servants until the will either turns
about or is turned. Most people never question the basis of the
assumptions on which they live and work. Their emotions go
unchecked and their thoughts move along on already prescribed
channels. Love is strong if it is released, and it contains the potential for reform. Love can overcome evil and destruction, but
only when the power of will endorses this goal too. Will must

first move reason into that line, and then both can reform the person by enabling love to flow outward freely, unmixed with self-satisfaction.

Until this point of transition is reached, no new life is possible. The old arguments simply go round and round. They can be refined and sophisticated, but not in such a way that people and the world are effectively altered and turned away from what is by nature a partially destructive course. When the will moves to separate love from its violent tendencies, God can be seen because the core of his nature is primarily such a power of reform. His core quality is that of being able naturally to love freely, and this cannot be disclosed fully by a rational analysis of the structure of nature and humanity. Both are on the whole locked into a combination constructive-destructive path.

Human beings are torn between a desire to love freely and an inability to reason themselves free of their primary self-concern, because reason has no such power to swing this delicate balance. When will desires its own reform and releases its power to support love's selfless side, then new life can open. The positive good we naturally seek becomes a possibility, but good first needs the backing of power before it can hope to overcome evil.

What is it about the human mind that makes it such a bad source of reform, in spite of Descartes' and Locke's hopes for its self-improvement projects? Why can reason perhaps explore its depths and structure, as Kant wanted, and yet not find the power to alter that structure? Much as it might want change, it ends only by accepting its present state. If we watch its natural tendencies, we see reason always working forward to exploit the dreams of the self. Or else, we see it work from past experience to repeat continually its defenses against its enemies and to develop apologies for its behavior. Of course, much supposed selfless desire to help another can be simply a concealed ambition to control and dominate, so that love requires close scrutiny too.

Thus, at least in this sense, the mind itself is "the slave of the passions," as Hume observed. It never of itself surrenders control or detaches its defenses from the self or admits its need for reform. It avoids this except in the sense of a need to perfect what it considers its basically correct technique. This is not to say that the mind may not reason well in science and mathematics, but it is to assert that, morally, it is not very often an ally of reform. Ironically, the emotions may be of more help to us here. We have argued that they have, if allowed, a basically more positive thrust toward the enhancement of good. On the other hand, reason argues just as effectively for destruction and evil as for the promotion of life. Kant is wrong; reason itself is amoral. Ethics of any noble sort is learned and purchased at the price of great personal reform.

Thus, reason will miss discovering the depth of emotion in God. It will discover him, if at all, as another mind. Or, in mystical fashion, the mind may announce its own limitations and inability to overcome the continual appearance of paradox and so argue to cancel all concentrated thought. When human will is given a chance to support the liberation of freely given love, God may become visible in this mode. Reason is given its place without transcending itself, and the reform of emotion appears as our prime need or goal.

Reason can now be released from its inordinate attachment to ego dreams and defensive strategy. Once detached, it can support the will in reforming the self by changing the inner direction of affection. This opens the person outward, something it would never occur to reason to do if left to itself. Left undisturbed, thought simply argues on, dreams on. Left unreformed, love simply connives to mask its passions under acceptable public acts. Reason continues to calculate quite correctly, but it also never escapes being the subtle instrument of the soul's desires. It loses its independent power to protest or reform. The desired new spirit can only spring up from the will's effect upon the emotions. But then the precarious moment comes: how can we keep the will from destroying all reason in its anger over being held in bondage? How then can we ease reason into a new league with a reformed or emptied emotional life?

B. The Steps

1. NEVER DEFEND YOURSELF: Obviously, this rule requires careful understanding before it can be accepted. If attacked by thieves, we should judge our own chances of protect-

ing our lives if we defend ourselves. If legally wronged or accused, whatever means of redress the courts allow certainly should be open to us. What is crucial for the project of self-reform is that we stop the enormous waste of energy that goes into explanations of the self. Our time is consumed protecting it against supposed slander, and our effort goes into all the justifications that constantly seek to boost our own image. That must all be stopped and turned.

Of course, some sensitivity to keeping up a public image is the essence of political life, so that one who desires personal reform cannot be engaged in private politics. Self-defense of this sort is self-defeating. The job is never done and thus requires constant and ever greater effort. Partly this is because the self is always encouraged to become even more sensitive to status and slight, but primarily it is because our energy is directed inward and thus continues to swirl around the self. All this forces reason into constant self-calculation. This blocks the outflow of love that is the essential directional change we need if reform is to take hold.

2. DEFEND ONLY DAMAGE TO ANOTHER: We want to encourage the outflow of love. If self-defense thwarts this, then moving out to defend only others in their attacks and in their needs will at least stimulate the right directional flow of emotion. It also encourages the power-support controlled by the will to join the right forces. Fierce self-concern constantly links the power of the will to desire vs. outbound love. This binds reason to the service of desire as it argues without any independent concern for good or evil. It also links emotion to the self without regard to its constructive or destructive orientation.

Life's most perplexing problem is the blind willingness of so many to take the whole world with them to destruction, if necessary, in order to defend themselves. We all know that an appeal to reason or to selfless moral purpose is useless as long as the will is linked with emotion in an iron determination to have its way over all else. To argue is as useless as to appeal to the common good. Once intelligence and emotion are directed to the outflow of love, the issue is: can the direction of the will be changed to support this? In vowing to defend only others and not yourself, the will is held oriented in an outward direction. In this way it is kept from bending all thought and desire to itself or to an inward concentration.

3. AVOID PLOTTING FUTURE DREAMS OR IMAGINING FUTURE DAMAGE: One reason our mind so seldom achieve any vision of God on its own is that the natural tendency is to dwell on past slights, future desires, and the imagined damage done by any who oppose us. If left alone, the mind will spend endless hours reasoning itself into an emotion of hate or anger. Sad to say, intelligence tends almost more to destruction than to construction, more to self-protection than to the encouragement of good. To imagine otherwise is to miscalculate the strength of the emotional and intellectual barriers that love faces.

Only if the will can turn to support love and block thought's tendency to move in self-defense is there any hope for either reform of the self or vision of God or new life. On this point Zen meditative practice is right but perhaps for the wrong reasons. It is necessary to block thought and alter it from its course, but this is not because the negative and positive forces of the world are locked in metaphysical balance. Rather, it is because unless altered by love and will, thought simply tends to increase desire further. Mental energy turns concentration constantly to the self by imagining future harm. Thus, our will must be employed to stop both the dreamy and paranoid tendencies that are unfortunately built into human thought.

4. EMPTY YOURSELF OF SELF-CONCERN WHETHER PAST, PRESENT, OR FUTURE: The Zen master knows that thought will not empty itself if left unopposed. Still our aim stops short of Zen. We concern ourselves not with emptying all thought, but simply with ousting those notions that dwell on exclusive self-concern, past, present or future. In order to do this, it may be necessary to induce a "dark night" when all thought and sensation are momentarily emptied in order that a new directional flow can be achieved. This emptying of thought and desire is undergone only in order to allow the will to exercise its power to accomplish a change of direction. It should move will toward the support of a love concerned for

others rather than for self. Love must be placed more in league with constructive good than with an evil or possessive spirit that moves to destruction too easily whenever it is opposed.

In the reform of self, reason cannot of itself be expected to do other than move in support of one's native desires. The effort of will, therefore, must be lent if we are to empty the mind of both thought and desire. Of course, as soon as life begins to move again the same selfish tendencies naturally reappear. This effort to empty the self of self-concern is never finished. The will must continually use the mind to stay on the alert in order to cut short all such tendencies as they emerge once again.

5. DEVELOP A ONE-WAY CONVERSATION WITH GOD: Most people who are religiously inclined tend to search for a dialogue with God. Or perhaps more modestly, they claim to listen for God's words. Ironically, this is essentially a selfish aim. Thus it has the religiously frustrating effect of defeating the movement for reform of the self because it blocks new life. That is, any pressing desire for divine conversation involves a concern of the self for itself and its own security. It is in essence ego inflating. God talks to us very little, because he knows that is the wrong direction for our attention. If God does flatter us with his words, this sometimes only locks us even more deeply into our ego-building project. We must learn to speak continually to him without desiring his constant support.

His silence is used to call us out, although of course if we fail to realize this, God's continued silence can also trap us in despair. But we must learn to speak without demanding that God flatter us with a reply. His words directed to us often only set us to repeating "what an important person am I." So many religiously possessed persons do this to the public disgrace of religion. If we can withstand self-imposed divine silence, and if we increase the outflow from the self and also learn more about God's outgoing nature, we can discern the reason for his failure to answer directly our constant demands. The Zen master won't respond directly. Why should God? Understanding God's use of silence gives us our best insight into his nature.

6. BECOME PERCEPTIVE ABOUT GOD'S POSSI-BLE MODES OF RESPONSE: God will not always speak

out, because he wants to develop an outward expression in us. Like many who teach by promoting indirect techniques, God may make use of various other signs, however. As one concerned to divert both our attention and our emotional flow from self-concentration, God will refuse to be bound to reply to us in any fixed or dependable pattern. Only thus can he hope to turn us from our human obsession to pin God down. We become fanatics in wanting to be sure of his response and intention. God is flexible not because he is quixotic by nature, or because he fears a human discovery of his intentions. It is only by refusing to be tied to a formula that he can escape being used as a means in the pursuit of what essentially are selfish human concerns.

Of course, if he adopts unorthodox tactics that are at odds with human desire, God risks our rejection. However, this dangerous course is also the only method that can hope to convert human beings away from their abuse of themselves and others due to their constant search for gratification. Learning to stay attentive to how and when and where God may choose to communicate himself to us keeps us constantly outer-directed in our sensitivity. Self-attention would only block our ability to sense God's love as freely flowing outward.

7. CULTIVATE THE TECHNIQUE OF PRESSURE AND PATIENCE: We first must make the discovery that God's direction is also outward, and thus he is not to be discerned fully by any inward search. Next we need to develop techniques appropriate to the discovery of a God who is revolutionary in his approach to the ordinary ways of humankind. If we constantly press to find his response, we only lose because that ends by placing attention back upon the demands of the self rather than away from it. On the other hand, if we abandon all pressure for discovery, we will never pierce the veil of the natural entanglements of human emotion. Abandoning all intensity is just as defeating as is the selfishness of pressing God constantly for the answer we seek.

We should move with persistence but with patience. Perhaps we need to alternate times of pressure for insight and change with contrasting periods of waiting for that moment propitious to alter emotion's flow and divert reason from its circular track. Again, no formula can be prescribed. Such certainty would allow us to manipulate God for our own satisfaction. This must be avoided at all costs, since it is self-defeating because it builds a wall against self-reform. All we can do is experiment continuously. Now we press for a breakthrough. Now we patiently withdraw pressure to see if the direction of love's flow will alter its course freely in the relaxation that comes after tension.

8. REMOVE ROADBLOCKS AND SEEK FULL EXPRESSION: If we cannot force the conversion of love, at least we can look out for the roadblocks that impede it. Some of these are hate, unforgiven ego wounds, constant attention to our own desires, etc. By doing this we work to unlock these emotions from their obsessive tendency because we refuse them our undivided attention. At the same time, we should not fail to increase our powers and creative talents to their maximum. Of course, there is a natural danger here of becoming a Narcissus by falling in love with one's own reflected beauty.

We must risk this. Obsessive humility and self-abasement are just as thwarting to change in love's flow as self-worship. We must love ourselves in order to love others and risk becoming stopped in self-admiration. One who demeans oneself sinks no less in self-concentration than one who is arrogant. A full and free self, openly expressing whatever creative talents it has, is the best candidate we have. It may allow the will to convert love to an outward flow, since all creation is impossible without some prior release from self.

9. ALLOW NEW LIFE TO BE BORN IN YOU: To be too self-depreciating about your native abilities is to risk rejecting the new life that might be born in you. You block its entrance by whining. To confess our faults opens us outward freely. To reject all creative powers in some supposed step of humility, however, is to stifle a talent given us and also to block God's possible entrance. As we become willing receptacles to what is inborn that seeks life in and through us, we give it birth outside of ourselves for the benefit of others. We no longer allow it simply to fester and decay inside, driving us to deeper self-concentration and lassitude.

Of course, allowing the birth of new life means not only

removing obstacles but diverting the will's power. The will should direct emotion and thought outward, even if the "outward" result is only a piece of paper now no longer void of words. "Allowing" means taming the will to be hospitable. It must not be constantly on a defensive alert, but we should encourage it to back the increase of good over evil by bending reason to that new course too. It takes effort and renewed vigilance to remain constantly open. Doors close with greater ease than they are opened, and they move back silently while unobserved.

10. ACCEPT FORGIVENESS AND NEVER DWELL ON MISTAKES: Again we must walk a tightrope. On the one hand, unless it is possible openly to admit mistakes, i.e., damage done to others, and move the will to desire a change, no new life is possible. On the other hand, almost as many human beings are crippled by excessive concentration on wrongs, whether real or imagined, and by their inability to accept forginveness as are inhibited by failing to develop a conscience. Thus, we should be willing to accept guilt, but we must also move on immediately to know that it can be forgiven because God cures himself of any defensive attention to inflicted wrongs.

We can join God and step beyond our tendency to dwell in remorse until we become sick. We can move on to restore life instead. To fret about sin is only one step better than to fret constantly about satisfying some selfish desire. But the hedonistic life is a step behind, because at least it is possible to move out to new life after dwelling for a time on remorse. On the contrary, it is not possible to move beyond self-directed love so long as self-satisfaction remains the unchallenged goal.

11. RESTORE YOUR LIFE BY RESTORING LIFE TO OTHERS: The hardest lesson to learn is that we cannot restore our own lives by direct attention. Thus we note the slightly self-defeating tendency encountered whenever we enter the psychiatrist's or the minister's office asking to have our damage repaired. The only way to find health is by seeking it in service or in a creative effort. This move actually turns the self away from the obsessive self-concentration that is the origin of most mild mental disorder. We have no powers of self-cure and

neither do others no matter how they are licensed. The task of removing self-concentration cannot be accomplished until it is abandoned.

If we stumble into restoring a life near us that is in need of repair, then, absorbed in this task, we necessarily are shaken loose from ourselves. While busy with another's concerns, we may discover the cure of self by the fact that we have unintentionally removed pressure and attention from it. The self as given must be emptied of content, but this cannot be done by allowing it the luxury of increased self-concern. It is sad to have money enough to force another to join you in self-concern. This is too bad because it buys off the very pressure that might force you to move in the only direction where health lies, i.e., outside the self in another's need.

12. BE ASSURED THAT GOD'S POWER IS SUF-FICIENT: Faith has been defined in many ways. Often it is confusingly connected to the demand for an intellectual assent to some creed. However right or harmless these verbal formulae may be in themselves, they in fact can block faith. We need to see that faith's essence means "the acceptance of the assurance that God's power is sufficient to reverse all human self-destructive tendencies and to allow new life to flow once love is given an outward direction." Of course, God's power requires instrumentation. We are dependent for his presence on people who can show us both forgiveness and a love directed to our needs and not theirs.

This is a rare event, and few treat us in this way. It can and does happen, and thus we must have the perception to recognize God's instrumentation wherever we find it. To trust those few events that appear to move against the normal flow of human passion—that is to have faith in God's control and in his ability to convert whom he chooses.

13. BE NOT CONTENT MERELY TO RECEIVE GOOD NEWS PASSIVELY: The experience of God's power to reform love and to change the will's direction is the "good news" Christianity constantly speaks about. The new life this brings into existence is only partially realized now. This lack of completion is all too evident in the world around us, and it is

even painfully dim in those who begin to experience such a directional change within themselves. Death means the extinguishing of hope. What "good news" reports is the availability of power to convert destruction to such an extent that life flows or is revived without internal or external impediment.

We cannot discover this by passively witnessing the changed tendencies either in ourselves or in saints. Only when the power of love is freed from its restrictions to self-gratification and becomes strong does our natural direction change so that we carry the message received out to others. Then the testimony is born and its effect witnessed in those who open themselves to such reversal. The renewed hope of new life made manifest is sufficient to make death and self-destruction move on their way to demise. Life increased is the "good news" to be spread, and at present it is the only sign we can see of power growing.

14. THE REVELATION OF SELFLESS LOVE REQUIRES ACTION: To find the self freed of its inner-directed and sometimes destructive desires is to realize the expressive power of outer-directed love. This new power may quite naturally find itself expressed in words, whether essay, story or song. One can witness to this change only by telling it in one's own way. Such a message may be an action in itself, just to the extent that the verbal form is powerful and capable of moving others to a similar saving experience. Words, too, sometimes rescue us when they convey love. Still, the nature of selfless love and its outward direction require a series of actions that move to embody that gift, which must happen if it is not simply to die again.

Love lives by being effectively transmitted. Most often "actions speak louder than words," particularly if one speaks of love but acts selfishly. The test that new life has been given to us is always the transformation of action. Outward-bound love, when not expressed, simply turns back into either destructive emotion or self-justifying thought. The first evidence that new life is being born is new action that conveys its vitality to others and supports life outside its source.

PART TWO

I

Sine Dolore Non Vivitur in Amore

A. Love without Pain

"There is no living in love without pain." We all know what love is. We have all had love given to us, and all of us have given love. We know its joy when we are loved; we also know its pain. We have loved our mothers and fathers and at times this hurt, although it could be blissful and fulfilling. We have all loved ourselves and found self-love not to be without its own pain. Some have even tried to love God and found that to be the most painful experience of all.

In bursts of religious optimism, we think all this might be different if only we could feel God's love. But we observe those in our age who are the most religiously possessed, and then we are sure that God's love, when it is felt, can raise pain to the limit of endurance. We all want love, but we seem to learn slowly that it cannot be acquired without pain. Once expressed and accepted, it becomes a joy and a pleasure. Yet, we are haunted by the understanding that to love or to be loved must first lead us back into pain.

Nevertheless, we hear the words of Paul in *Romans*, and we want to believe that "all things work together for good for those who love the Lord" (King James translation). To those of us pained by love, this sounds like the release we need, and such freedom is at the heart of the Christian promise. How are we to understand this beautiful offer? And more important, how can we individually appropriate it in order to escape the pain involved in love? How can we move love out beyond pain?

One problem is that our own needs cause us to focus on the situation stated in the first part of Paul's phrase, and then we avoid thinking of the mystery involved in the last part. That is,

123

we cling to saying, "All things work together for good," and we avoid the restrictive clause "for those who love the Lord." We sometimes have trouble loving ourselves, let alone our family or our neighbor, and they are all too nearby. What in heaven's name could it mean to "love God," or even to "love Jesus," both of whom are now so hard for us to see? Yet perhaps the secret of how love can go beyond pain lies in solving the puzzle of how and what it means to "love God."

To understand the inner or the spiritual human life has never been easy, but we unfortunately are a generation who seem to have forgotten all the rules. Whenever we struggle free from the physical blindness sex can induce, we know that love is, on the whole, something unseen. It is a matter of the inner life. Thus, if we are to understand the sources of love, there is no alternative except for each of us to explore his or her own spiritual life. And as if that were not enough, standing beyond is the terror of the love of God. However, there seems to be no way to press love beyond pain except by exploring our interior depths and thus risking a confrontation with God. Those who report being found by God have never had easy lives, and yet sometimes this experience has also placed them beyond the reach of pain.

The love of God brings with it demands for change in our nature which will not leave us the same, should God choose to touch us as we seek him. Yet, we know the same is true of human love. Either to experience or to give it changes us, and part of our pain comes from knowing we will never be quite the same after submitting to love as before. Love of others demands the loss of the self, but self-surrender never comes easily or without its pain. We want love, but we fear the loss involved in change. Perhaps we are no longer able to enjoy what once we did so easily, but this failure to achieve our preset goals eventually pales in comparison, once love is through tearing at us.

The love of God may move us not to sheer good but out to some no-man's-land beyond good and evil where God dwells. Once we overcome our natural romanticism, we realize both the demands that love involves and the dangers that a closeness to God brings with it. Thus, anyone who understands love will never again utter lightly, "All things work together for good for those who *love* the Lord" (King James translation; italics mine). To speak the word "love" is to say something hard.

After all, Jesus loved both God and us, and look what happened to him. God loved him, or so Jesus never doubted, but a love like that does not shrink from the test of pain. To love requires our involvement and commitment to the lives of others, which is never an easy thing. Just as Jesus bore our suffering, so all who love or are loved must bear an extra burden along with their joy. To love God and to share his torment as he looks over the affairs of humanity—that is to feel a love that is divine. It is also an emotion sometimes too much for human frailty to bear.

To love the Lord is to "work for the good," so it is said; but how many good causes do you know that come off easily? Augustine says that all people can be divided into two groups according to the direction of their affections. One type is more interested in the self, or in causes that, however noble, are simply an extension of self. The other type is capable of setting self aside and directing affection to another's need, which is the same as to say loving God.

Here is the definition of what Christian ministry means and here also are the depths of Christian love. It seeks more to minister to another than simply to attend to its own needs. The issue is: are we attracted to a religious path simply in order to be ministered unto? Or, on the other hand, do we seek a way of release from our self-infatuation in order to listen to a need other than our own? To turn away from the world and to seek God is, in the Christian experience, to suceed only in being driven back from the gates of heaven toward the wasteland on earth. Human self-interest is destroyed by the force of God's love. It turns us around to face needs immediately at hand. We are told to offer a kind word, a cup of cold water, and to lose ourselves in that experience.

On first encounter, the love of God may be destructive due to the terror of its impact on us. However, the Christian believes this loss produces new life once the cord of our fierce attachment to our own interest is cut. Isn't that why we call Jesus a "savior," because he suffered silently, without protest, for our needs and not for his own noble causes? Neither Pilot nor his spears could force a word of protest from Jesus' lips. He made his life ours; he did not demand that we make our lives his, although we may do so in response to love.

Yet, mystery of mysteries, Christians have been bidden to be joyful. How can we feel joy, now, today, when we find the love of God so painful? "To worship" means to praise God for what he has done. He has at times been kind to Christians and Jews, but the overwhelming blindness and destruction of humanity made Jesus weep over Jerusalem. And God's tears in Noah's day were deep enough to cover the face of the earth with water, so it is reported. If love is like that, Christians have real need to huddle together for worship—which means to renew our joy—if we hope to keep hold of the Christian promise that love can move beyond pain. Worship should never be based on a shallow joy; that would ignore how painful the love of God is and how deep the rivers of deception flow outside any church's doors. We need to sing hymns together in order to keep our spirits up. We worship in order to renew the promise given in the rainbow that love can one day come without pain.

If to live in love is to invite pain, so that some turn cold to love in order to avoid its afflictions; and if to set out on the road to love God is to risk the destruction of our most cherished selves and to expose the soul to the terrors of many a dark night —then on what ground do we gather together to sing hymns of praise? How can worship mean "giving thanks to God for inaugurating the day when love will be without pain" when almost every present experience denies this? The world around us always threatens to burst in the doors of our temples and to destroy our altars. It takes a lot of nerve to "praise God from whom all blessings flow" when we must pay the price of love with an almost equal amount of pain. But then, perhaps it takes a lot of nerve to be a Christian and to deny that the pain we all experience in love is the final word.

Of course, Jesus' disciples recovered from their agony over his death only because God's intervening action took them by surprise and restored Jesus to them when they thought him lost. All later Christian joy stems from that moment, since up to that point Jesus' life simply went down the road from celebration to crucifixion. Still, the disciples' post-Easter joy was short-lived —just as ours often is—because Jesus' presence was soon withdrawn from them again. For every resurrection of life there is later ascension, that is, a moving away from human life.

Like us, those early Christians continued living confident that their joy would return permanently at any moment. They proved to be wrong in their immediate expectation, just as we are often wrong in predicting a permanent change for the better. Yet their lives of expectation were amazingly charged with power and so became marvelously fruitful. Does this mean that *the expectation of new life is just as powerful a force as the full descent of pure bliss*? I think so.

To be a Christian is to live constantly on a wing and a promise, always in youthful expectation that a day will come when love will be pure and beyond pain. To be a Christian means always to be painfully sensitive that the world and people are rarely that way, that love among human beings is just as destructive as it is fulfilling. Is there no way for Christians now to share in what they expect to be God's dramatic inbraking future shock?

To live with that question is to know the anxiety of the Christian life. We know—whatever else is true—that such love cannot come to exist in the present day without our first facing the terror of the search for God and the sure loss of our own pride and ambition that result from such a meeting. Love without pain can be given and received; that is what we mean by the sense of God's indwelling presence. The Holy Spirit hides from zealots' pride in their own actions, but it can show itself in rare moments when we give ourselves away to some immediate, perhaps simple, human need. The big issues are seldom the Christian issues, however important they may be otherwise.

The physical needs of our time are, as ever, enormous. But the spiritual needs of those who find themselves stripped bare today are so overwhelming that they portend a vast spiritual wandering and search in America, one that has already begun. Still, whenever the dark night of the soul arrives, God also may be near at hand, if we are sensitive enough to distinguish his prodding from the devils that torment us.

Ours is a day that knows suffering, but the question is whether we should turn in frustration and thrust it upon everyone who will listen. Or, if it is to be religiously effective for change, must suffering be internally borne? To announce one's suffering publicly may be simply another form of egotism, whereas the only cure for our inner suffering may be to set it aside along with our own pride. In that moment we are at last free to turn and minister to the suffering near at hand. We only learn to listen after we realize our shouting is no longer of any avail. Christianity begins at home, and it is as near as the person next to us, if only we can reach out and touch that person.

To bear silently the pain involved in love may be the very meaning of non-self-centered love, and perhaps internal silence is the only way to heal suffering rather than to increase it. Yet, what of the future that is said to be brighter than this bleak picture and is promised to us by the vision reported in *The Book of Revelation* (21:1-5)? Yes, we need a new creation; human renewal is way overdue. Christianity in its powerful moments has been more joyful than merely advising us to learn to heal others by bearing our own suffering silently. Christianity moves beyond hope. Yet we must never forget, as we reach out eagerly for the Christian promise of love without pain, that this day will not fully appear until the world is radically altered. Hope cannot by itself culminate in painless love. Human beings hope, but love still depends on God for its day of fulfillment.

A new day will arrive only when God comes out of hiding and lives with his human creatures. The lion and the lamb may lie down together on that day, but right now they are at each other's throats. *To be a Christian is to bring as much of that future joy of love into the present condition of humanity as pain permits.* In this way we do show forth God's love till he comes again. If we can do that even for a time, we have good reason to gather together to worship and to praise God. We give thanks to him for allowing us to bring his future promise into the present lives of those around us. To experience love's fulfillment ought to draw Christians together to sing hymns of praise.

B. To Minister Unto

Jesus is quite clear about his own relationship to other people, and also about the relationship that all who are his disciples should assume. He came not to be ministered unto, but rather to minister to the needs of others. The direction of his attention is outward and away from himself and not toward his own satisfaction or attempted spiritual increase. Of course, he is also clear about the fact that benefits accrue to those who can absorb themselves in the needs of others. The point is that all self-improvement and release (salvation) comes by directing attention away from the self, rather than by an intensive exploration of its depths following some prescribed ritual.

Like most important issues affecting the spirit, this question is more complicated than any neat division into inner vs. outer direction. We know from watching our children, or ourselves as children, that the means the self can devise for calling attention to itself are many and subtle. The most ingenious of these takes the form of a supposed noble concern for others, which at the same time has the sly side effect of directing attention to ourselves and to what noble and generous people we are. When we are successful in this plot, our selves can design any show of concern so that it is impossible for others to fail to acknowledge us as heroes. That is, they are forced to admire us unless they also deny their legitimate relief of suffering. By calling attention to some wrong in need of redress, we succeed in directing the bulk of attention toward our own self-sacrificing selves.

Does Jesus offer any remedy for this tricky situation? If not, our only alternative is to reject some legitimate heroes in order to avoid over-inflating the ego that comes attached to the sacrificial act. One clue, I suggest, is to watch how suffering is borne in the Gospel accounts and when protest is made. One's own suffering, Jesus' model would seem to indicate, should be internally borne and not externalized. In this way the issue is not clouded by our own protest of personal injustice. Jesus bears internally his own problems. He uses them as a tool to deepen his reflection and sensitivity. His protest becomes vocal and public only when *someone else* is hurt and is in need of aid. Still, the trick is to do this in such a way that attention is focused on the wrong done and not on the person of the protester.

Religiously, one stands alone, or perhaps before God if one can stand that. We often sense this interior isolation in Jesus' words. However, the aim of his religious interiorization is to increase the effectiveness and the power of words and actions when finally they do come out. The aim is to direct attention to its real target and away from the protesting self. Furthermore, some announced protests only aggravate the situation, so that their effect is to increase human suffering rather than to release it. When this happens, it is clear that the public fuss serves only to release energy in the protester rather than to relieve any public agony. The motive and the effect of any protest are the crucial considerations that should govern our public expressions.

Those called to minister, which is Jesus' challenge to us, should govern their actions by the effect they will have upon the people served. Of course, this can easily become an excuse for a rigid conservatism, one that never places any controversial burden on the conscience of those one seeks to help. But again Jesus' actions are clear; he never shrinks from calling his followers to harder tasks. In fact, his mission is to bring them unmistakably face-to-face with God's demands. Yet in each case, one can see that the effect aimed for is spiritual growth and release of power—if only the listener will yield and accept such a burden. The key issue becomes whether the receivers of the protest are shattered by the charge laid upon them, or whether they are drawn to greater effectiveness.

The aim of all public protest, then, should be to increase our interior struggle in ways that lead to greater depth and an increased ability to help others. To do this, rather than to confuse one's listener, requires a skill in spiritual direction. Simple moral injunctions without increased spiritual guidance lead to little of religious consequence. Moralizing must be judged strictly on the basis of its political effectiveness. Since Jesus' aim first of all is to lead his followers to greater depths of spiritual insight, we must place any public protest of wrongs within that context. People were first attracted to Jesus because he gave spiritual aid and relieved suffering, not because his political reform movement was exciting. Of course some Jews misunderstood his program and were disappointed because they expected political changes he never claimed to provide.

Perhaps the secret lies in the fact that we are able to heal suffering only if we know what unannounced and internally borne suffering means, due to self-enforced personal silence. A popular cause moves directly to rally support to itself, but the ministry of Christianity is never simply a popular protest, however worthy the cause may be. In this context, every protest raised is first of all an attempt to minister to the individual and to use suffering as a sensitizing source in order to heighten one's ability to respond to the needs of others. Therefore, if any public protest simply works to drive the listener deeper into self in confusion and self-concentration, we can be sure it is not a Christian cause however legitimate it may be on other grounds.

Again we return to the centrality of the Christian theme of love. We know that love made manifest will seldom be without pain. However, if we consider every public protest we make and every burden we lay upon others within the context of demonstrated love, then we can call the action "Christian." That is, the recipients of the burden laid upon them by our actions or words are at the same time aware that the suffering involved and the sacrifice called for are placed upon them in a spirit of love and concern for their own religious maturity. And it is amazing how easy it is to tell whether the injunctions given to us spring primarily from the speaker's self-interest, or whether they stem from loving concern for our spiritual liberation. That distinction is all important to the health of any religious life.

How can love be applied in a Christian attempt to minister to human needs while we still remain free to protest against the evils of the day? The rule of prior repentance and forgiveness is crucial. That is, if the words or actions of the would-be minister of relief simply increase the emotional tension among those who receive aid, no change in life—the Christian is convinced—can come about. Anyone caught in a net of destructive acts must move to repent those actions that increase suffering and seek both forgiveness and a change in orientation. Factually speaking, Christian public protest must be judged by whether it is effective in drawing repentance from its hearers. If it is not, it is just one more power pressure play of the day.

Thus, any Christian attempt aims to direct the hearer's attention toward God in confession and in a request for a forgiveness that will change one's action. If the attention goes anywhere else first except to God, it may be politically effective or even socially desirable, but it is not Christian in its thrust. The belief is that no substantial change can come, no sustained relief from suffering is possible, until the individual acknowledges the wrong direction of his or her efforts and feels the receipt of God's forgiving power. It is easy to match protest against protest and power against power; it is extraordinarily difficult to lead a person into the genuine desire to find a newly directed life.

Thus, if we place political or social-action campaigns on one side and the mystical withdrawal for contemplation on the other, Christianity floats illusively in between. That is, Christians have an affinity with the goal of all mystics to break through the natural bonds that restrict the self in order to find a fuller spiritual life that lies beyond or beneath. Christianity joins every mystic in being unsatisfied with the human person as given, and seeks ways to liberate the self to wider spiritual expression. However, since Christianity's first aim is to minister to the needs of others and not simply to pressure for its own satisfaction, it joins all activists in wanting oppressive structures broken. Thus, individual Christians can never withdraw completely or remove themselves entirely from the scene of social and political combat.

If Christian effort is successful, the self is transformed, but it is not transcended. God is also more profoundly understood, but he too remains a self opposed to the self of the religious seeker. There must be a center left to a person if one is to repent and seek forgiveness, and there must also be a self in God with the power of will if he is to remain himself while exercising the power to forgive and transform others. As with every mystical doctrine, the natural human being cannot understand how this occurs. Thus, our need is to reach an enlightenment beyond the natural self. How is this attained and what happens to the self in the process? This is the issue Christianity must answer in order to define itself against other religious doctrines.

Perhaps one key to the effectiveness of every Christian ministry, and the right basis for every social protest, lies in the Great Commandment: to love God with all your heart and your neighbor as yourself. That is, love toward God is the first goal, and it takes precedence even over compassion toward suffering. Again, the Christian should reject any mystical fixation that centers solely on relating the self to God, because we must consistently stress the love of other human beings as necessarily coordinate. On the other hand, we cannot forget that every move to relieve suffering in a Christian context requires us to solve the perplexing problem of God's nature and how and what it means for people to love God with all their hearts and minds. That is an amazing task, as the mystic knows, but it is also a necessary prelude to every overt act of mercy.

Every social protest seeks to induce a change. Yet it is the Christian conviction that no effective change comes about in people's lives except through their own experience of what God's love means. Such love is not without its terror. Every mystic who lives through the "dark night" of inner purgation—or every Jesus abandoned on a cross—will testify to that. We are changed by "knowing Jesus," as our evangelical friends say. This can happen to us not because of his words but insofar as we live our lives through the heights and the depths to which God's love carried Jesus. However, we must couple this with a willingness to expose ourselves to similar purification. God's love is at first hidden, and so it must be sought for intensively.

The secret of all sustained Christian ministry, then, lies in penetrating the subtle relationship that holds between love and pain, joy and hope. We cannot deny that love pains us now, particularly the love of God, which is so absolutely demanding. Yet the Christian hope is based in a promise that the suffering that love normally involves will eventually be overcome. Jesus' love for his people led to his crucifixion. Our present joy stems from the hope that love can one day be without pain, just as crucifixion did not end Jesus' life, even if a total transformation of humanity and the world is required to make this possible. Ultimately, the basis of Christian belief does not rest in hope alone, which would be simply to hope against hope. Ironically, faith in love beyond pain must center in love itself as it is now experienced, even the terror of the love of God.

How can Christians base their hope on love when our only experience of love now includes its involvement with pain, e.g., Jesus crucified? To understand this we must return to the central call of John the Baptist: repent for the kingdom of God is at hand. The "Pure Land" is near; every mystic knows that it dwells within us, even though undisclosed to most. The peculiar Christian experience joins that of the mystic in seeking inner transformation, but it also includes the experience of feeling the forgiveness of God's love, which in this case heals and removes pain. Luther struggled through pain but finally felt forgiveness and was transformed. To be moved to ask for forgiveness, and at some moment to feel God's love granting this without pain or condition—that is the center of the Christian life. And it is also the basis for any belief that love lies beyond both hope and pain.

II

A vs. B

A. There is no living in love without pain.

Latin Proverb

B. And we know that in everything God works for good with those who love him.

Romans 8:28 (RSV)

III
The Steps

1. NEVER DEFEND YOURSELF.

2. DEFEND ONLY DAMAGE TO ANOTHER.

3. AVOID PLOTTING FUTURE DREAMS OR IMAGINING FUTURE DAMAGE.

4. EMPTY YOURSELF OF SELF-CONCERN WHETHER PAST, PRESENT OR FUTURE.

5. DEVELOP A ONE-WAY CONVERSATION WITH GOD.

6. BECOME PERCEPTIVE ABOUT GOD'S POSSIBLE MODES OF RESPONSE.

7. CULTIVATE THE TECHNIQUE OF PRESSURE AND PATIENCE.

8. REMOVE ROADBLOCKS AND SEEK FULL EXPRESSION.

9. ALLOW NEW LIFE TO BE BORN IN YOU.

10. ACCEPT FORGIVENESS AND NEVER DWELL ON MISTAKES.

11. RESTORE YOUR LIFE BY RESTORING LIFE TO OTHERS.

12. BE ASSURED THAT GOD'S POWER IS SUFFICIENT.

13. BE NOT CONTENT MERELY TO RECEIVE GOOD NEWS PASSIVELY.

14. THE REVELATION OF SELFLESS LOVE REQUIRES ACTION.